THE
FIRST WEEKS
OF LIFE

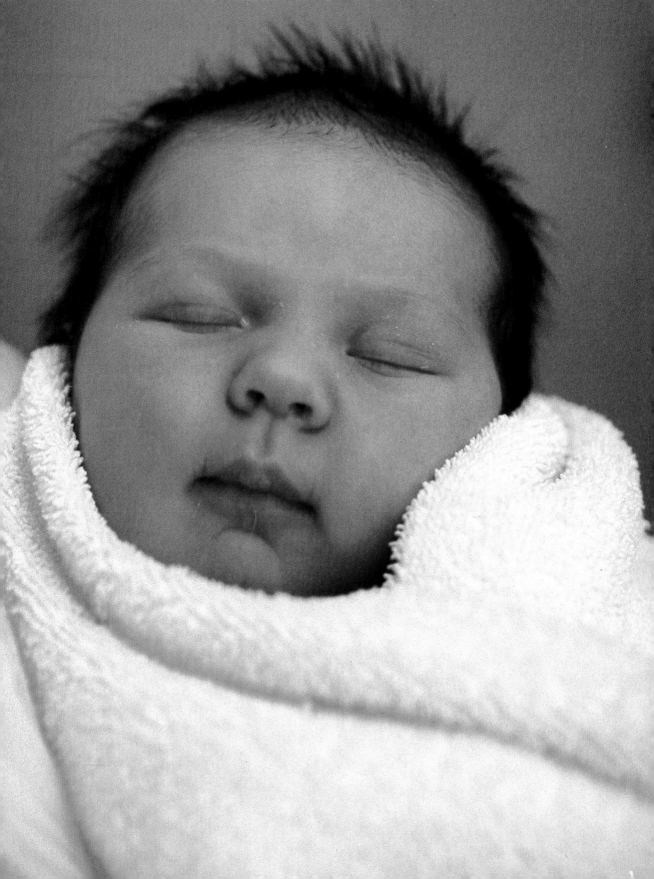

THE FIRST WEEKS OF LIFE

MIRIAM STOPPARD
MD MRCP

Photography by
NANCY DURRELL MCKENNA

BALLANTINE BOOKS · NEW YORK

For Oliver, Barnaby, William and Edmund

Editor Ricki Ostrov
Designed by Anne Cuthbert
Editorial Director Amy Carroll
Managing Art Editor Denise Brown

Library of Congress Cataloging-in-Publication Data

Stoppard, Miriam.
    The first weeks of life / Miriam Stoppard : photography by Nancy
Durrell McKenna.—1st American ed.
        p.   cm.
    "First published by Dorling Kindersley Limited in Great Britian in 1989"
Bibliography: p.
Includes index.
ISBN 0-345-36027-3
    1. Infants (Newborn)—Care—Popular works. I. Title.
RJ253.S82   1989   89-6487
649'.122—dc19   CIP

Manufactured in the United States of America

First American Edition: March 1990

10 9 8 7 6 5 4 3 2 1

INTRODUCTION

The old Jesuit adage, give me a child until he's seven then he will be mine, implied that a person's most formative years were those up to seven years of age. During the time I was qualifying as a doctor it decreased to three years old, then two, then one. It soon fell again to six months, by when, it was believed, that a child had learned the most basic rules of human behavior in terms of relating to others — friendliness, hostility, the rules of dialogue, etc.

In the last decade with advancing technology and more careful observation, researchers realized that five and six-week-old babies are striving to communicate with smiles, waves, and attempts at conversation.

Most recently we've discovered that neo-natal babies can recognise the sight of mother's face in less than a week. More importantly, they are beginning to bond to the smell and sound of parents 24 hours after birth. And although they can't change the length of focus of their eyes, they can see anything which is the magic 8–10 inches away — the distance of their fixed focal lengths.

Babies chatted to, especially in a high-pitched sing-song voice (all that baby-talk has a biological function), speak more fluently and read earlier than those who are deprived of a running commentary. Songs and clapping games only improve matters. And in this connection it's salutary to remember that baby birds who fail to hear bird song before six weeks of age will NEVER sing.

Learning starts from birth plus one second, and the steepest part of a baby's learning curve is the first six weeks ..... six days ..... six hours ...... Without being aware of this in the first few weeks of life, and consciously acting on it, we could be curtailing the chance of our children developing to their full potentials and failing in one of the most crucial parental roles — that of teacher.

CONTENTS

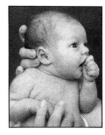

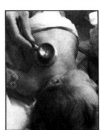

CHANGES IN YOU

FEEDING YOUR BABY

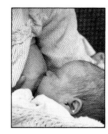

TAKING CARE OF YOUR BABY

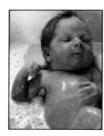

BEING AT HOME

RECORD OF THE BIRTH

Did you have the baby in the hospital? ....

Did contractions begin spontaneously? ....

    or were you induced?...

Date and time contractions began

    Date .... Time ....

Where were you?..

Who was with you? ....

Their reaction? ....

Initially, how far apart were your contractions?

....

How long did each one last? ....

At what time did you call the doctor?....................................

What instructions were you given?...

....

At what time did you reach the hospital? ....

How far apart were the contractions then?................................

How many centimeters were you dilated? ....

Did your membranes rupture spontaneously? ....

    or were they ruptured by the doctor? ....

Who was in attendance: doctor? .... nurse? ....

Were you given the following: sleep medication? ....

    muscle relaxants? .... painkillers? ....

tranquilizers? .... labor stimulants? ....

anesthetics? ....

Was an IV used? ....

Was a fetal monitor used? .... internal ....

    external .... If so, for how long? ....

How long were you in labor for

    the first stage? ....

    the second stage? ....

    the third stage? ....

In what position did you give birth: lying down? ....

    sitting up? .... standing? ....

Was the baby born head first? .... or breech? ....

Was he/she in the posterior (face up) position?......................

    or anterior (face down) position?..

Were forceps used?...

Did you have an episiotomy? ....

    any tears? .... stitches? ....

Did you have a cesarean?

How long did the delivery take?...

Did the baby need any special resuscitation? ....

Did he/she need intensive care of any kind?

....

What was the baby's Apgar score 1 minute after birth?

.... 5 minutes after birth? ....

When did you first nurse the baby? ....

Did the baby nurse well?..

....

Did you have to follow a schedule?.....................................

Did you have rooming-in?...

Was the baby separated from you? ....

    How soon after birth?..

Did the baby develop any problems in the hospital? ....

....

....

    in the first two weeks at home?...

....

....

Did the baby get jaundiced?..

What treatment was applied?...

....

Did you have any complications during the labor?...............

....

after the birth?...

....

Were there any problems with the expulsion of the

placenta?

....

Did you hemorrhage or bleed heavily after the birth?.........

....

Did you have any infections associated with childbirth?

....

with breastfeeding?...

How long did you stay in the hospital?...................................

NOTES

_____

_____

_____

_____

_____

_____

_____

_____

BABY'S FIRST APPEARANCE

BOY .... WEIGHT ....

GIRL .... LENGTH ....

BORN AT .... HEAD SHAPE AT BIRTH ....

DATE .... HAIR COLOR ....

TIME .... BIRTHMARKS ....

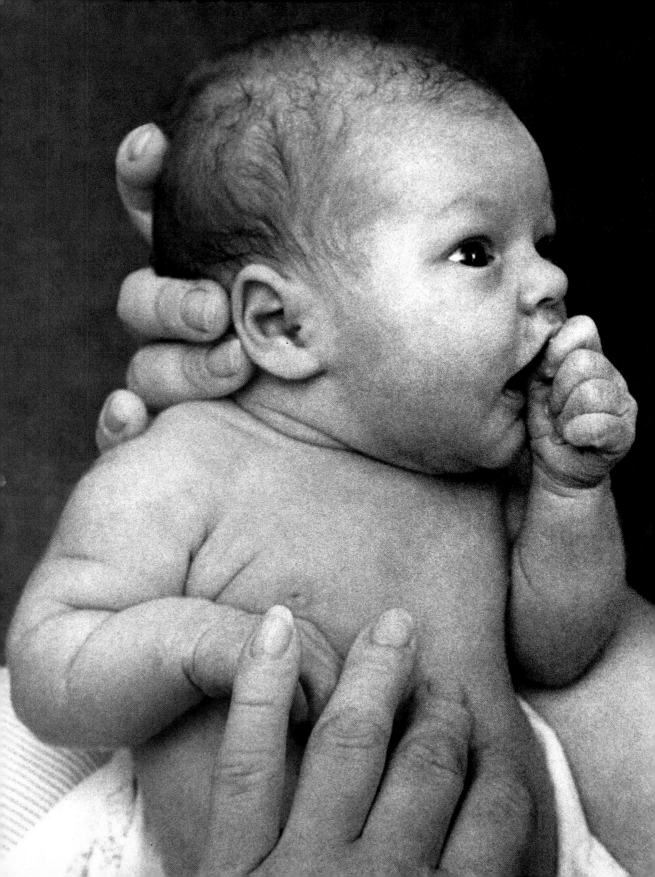

1

YOUR BABY'S APPEARANCE

You have labored hard and at last your baby is here. Only minutes ago she was laid in your arms. You feel that you held her for what seemed to be the briefest time while you looked her over and counted her fingers and toes. Now she's being weighed and you begin to worry. Is she all right? What has she got all over her? Isn't she a funny color? Why is her head that shape? What is that hair she has all over herself?

Almost certainly you've never seen such a young baby before, and your baby may look somehow different than you expected. Most newborn babies do look a little peculiar, but rarely is this a cause for worry. Both the baby's physical immaturity, and the birth process itself, are responsible for most of the things about which you may be surprised or apprehensive. It takes a while — up to two weeks — for a baby's body to begin to adjust to life outside the uterus.

Don't be surprised if nobody else seems concerned. Doctors and nurses have seen many newborn babies and are very used to their appearances. But if there is anything that worries you, don't hesitate to ask about it. All mothers want to know their babies are normal.

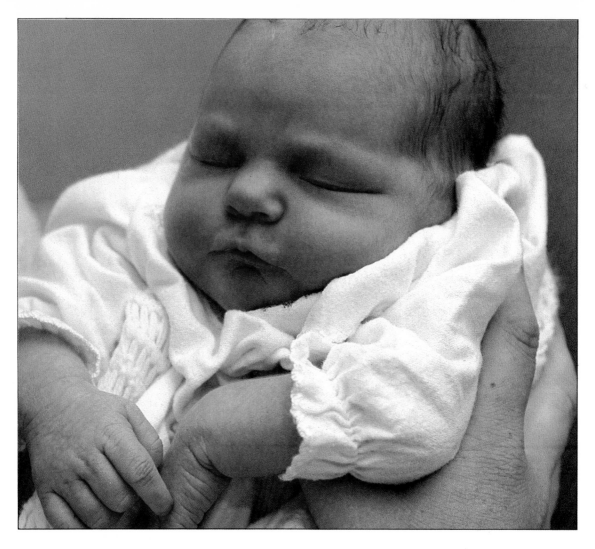

SIZE

During an initial examination your doctor will measure your baby's weight and head circumference. He or she may also measure the baby's length. The measurements are really taken to form a base-line for your baby's future development to no one but herself. She must not be compared with other babies of the same age. Another reason for taking this measurement is for averages, and you know very well that there is no such thing as an average baby, so take all these measurements in your stride.

The average weight of a baby at birth is about 7lb 3oz but large variations occur depending on genetic, racial, nutritional and placental factors, among others. The more weight you gain during pregnancy, the larger your baby is likely to be. Taller, heavier, older (over 24), and diabetic mothers, and those who carried their babies for extended periods, tend to have larger babies. If you suffered from certain conditions such as pre-eclampsia, chronic hypertension, vascular or renal disease or smoked

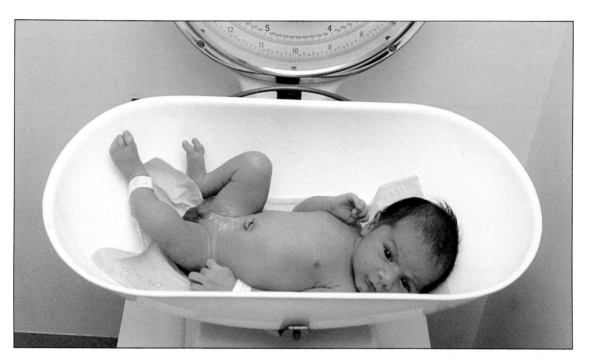

ABOVE AND RIGHT
Shortly after birth a number of developmental checks are carried out. Your baby's weight and length will be recorded and her head circumference will be measured. These will provide an indication of your baby's development.

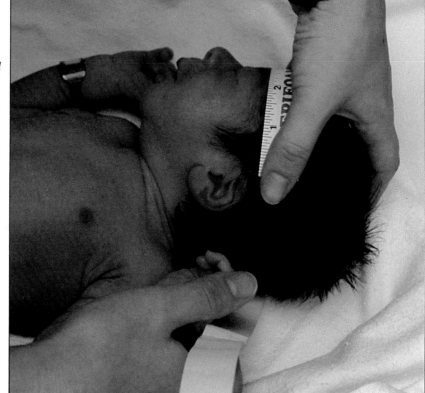

OPPOSITE
Your baby's head will appear disproportionately larger than the rest of her body; it is about one-quarter of her entire length. Her eyelids may be reddish and swollen due to the pressure of the birth process. This swelling usually disappears in a day or two.

during pregnancy, your baby is likely to be lighter in weight. Girls generally weigh less than boys. Twins and triplets are usually smaller than singly-born infants.

Babies born around their expected time weigh between 5lb 8oz and 9lb 12oz. Don't worry if your baby is on the small side. My second son was born at 6lb 4oz and he's brighter than the lot of us.

Normally your baby will lose weight during the first three or four days following birth because she takes some time to feed consistently. Weight loss at this time is usually about 4–6oz. (But it's still considered normal for babies to lose up to 10 per cent of their birth weights.) Then she will have one or two days of stable weight followed in the sixth day by a weight increase that, over a week, averages 6oz. A baby's weight gain is the most important way of determining the adequacy of her food intake, and her overall physical state.

The average length of a baby at term is 19–20in, but once more, large variations can occur.

The average head circumference is about 14in (35cm) and a newborn's head is disproportionally larger than the rest of her body, comprising about one-fourth of her entire length. The head often appears lopsided, pointed or flattened. This is caused by the baby's skull being molded by the confines of the birth canal as she passes through. The younger the baby is, the larger her head is in proportion: a premature baby's head is an even greater percentage of her overall size. As a baby gets older one of the dramatic changes to her body proportions is that her head seems to get smaller but all it means is that her body is growing very fast to catch up with the development of her head and brain.

The circumference of your newborn baby's chest will be smaller than that of her head. Her stomach may appear surprisingly large and rounded, due to the weakness of her abdominal muscles, when compared to her very small hips and buttocks.

Many newborns fall asleep just after birth. This may be the result of medication given to the mother. Because of the restricted space in the mother's body, the legs are somewhat bowed at birth, and both these and the arms are short in relation to the body length. Many babies remain curled up in the fetal position for several days, with their fists clenched and their arms and legs held close to their body.

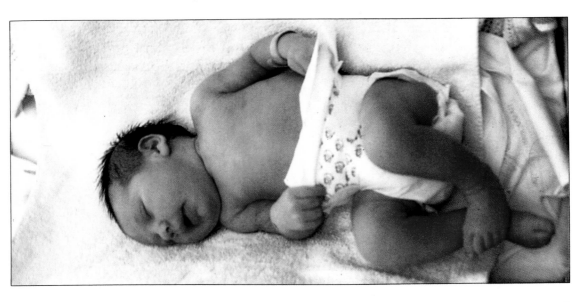

Your baby may look different than you expected immediately after birth. Her skin may be damp, red and blotchy, and she may be covered with vernix, the greasy substance that covered her body and protected her skin from the amniotic fluid.

Your baby may have lots of hair on her head and be covered with fine downy hair on her body. This body hair will rub off in the weeks after birth. She may also cry immediately after birth. This is nothing to worry about, and the action helps to clear her lungs and respiratory system of mucus and fluid.

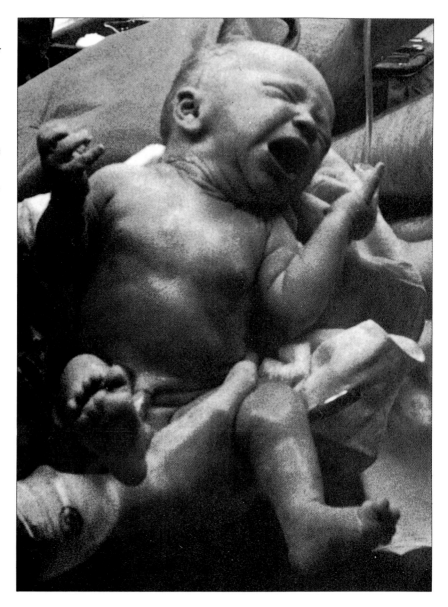

VERNIX

Don't be put off if your baby seems to be covered with a grayish, whitish, yellowish, greasy, cheesy substance. This is vernix and your baby is covered with it to protect her skin from becoming water-logged by amniotic fluid during the time she spent in the uterus. Some babies have this greasy substance spread all over their entire bodies and faces, while others have it only on isolated parts like their faces and hands. The presence of vernix is one reason why a newborn baby is so slippery and difficult to handle.

Hospital practice in relation to vernix varies. In some hospitals it is left on for a time because it provides a natural barrier against minor skin infections, in others it is cleaned off at birth. If vernix is not cleaned off, it comes off by itself within two or three days. Look out for large accumulations of vernix in the skin folds that may cause irritation and should be wiped away.

FONTANELLES

The fontanelles in a way are the windows into a baby's body. These are the soft spots in the top of the baby's head in the space where the skull bones have not yet joined; they don't fuse until your baby is about two years old. The bones of the skull don't fuse because the softness of the skull actually protects the brain. Also there can be rapid changes of pressure inside your baby's head which unfused bones easily accommodate.

Because the head is large in comparison to the body, and is usually first down the birth canal, the fontanelles allow the soft skull bones to mold (that is, to ride over one another) without damage to the baby's brain as she passes through the narrow birth canal. The fontanelles are covered by the baby's scalp and a tough membrane but you may be able to feel or see her fontanelles pulsating. You do not need to take any special care of them, but you should make sure that they are never pressed very hard.

Fontanelles can vary greatly in size and there are no standard dimensions. However, the fontanelle may become concave when your baby is short of water and may become convex if the pressure inside the head is increased. If you ever notice that there is a bulge or if the area is abnormally shrunken, you should contact your doctor immediately.

SKIN COLOR

We use the phrase soft as a baby's bottom to describe something very delicate, silky and smooth and the skin of a newborn is tender and easily damaged. While your baby is still inside the uterus her skin is a pale pink. At the time of delivery most babies are a pinkish blue or purple color. The bluish discoloration, known as cyanosis, is caused by a temporary lack of oxygen at the time of birth. As soon as your baby is breathing her color will change to pink – first her lips, then the skin around her mouth, then her body followed soon after by the rest of her face. Her arms and legs do not change color until after her body has become completely pink. Last of all to pinken are her hands and feet, which remain a pale bluish color for several minutes or occasionally several hours. It is quite natural for your baby's skin to appear blotchy and it may change color very quickly. Feel your baby to see if she is too hot or too cold and take appropriate action but don't worry about small color changes, they are normal.

You may notice that the top half of your baby's body may be pale while the lower half is red. This is due to her immature circulation, which causes blood to pool in her lower limbs. Moving your baby around will correct this difference in skin color. Babies that will have a dark skin do not always do so at birth. Melanin, the body's natural pigment, is not present in the skin immediately. It takes weeks or months before the final shade is present.

JAUNDICE

Jaundice – a yellowish coloration of the skin and the whites of the eyes is really quite common. Many healthy newborn infants develop a yellow coloring of the skin on about the third day of life. Known as physiological jaundice, it is not a disease but is due to the baby's blood

Few newborn babies look perfect. You might notice your baby has patches of dry skin (right), irregular skin coloration and scratches (far right) or reddish swollen eyes (below). All of these conditions are harmless and clear up soon after birth.

A baby's fingernails can be long and sharp. Some babies are born with scratches caused by their own nails while in the uterus. Sometimes a baby's thumb is red and wrinkled, indicating it was sucked in the uterus.

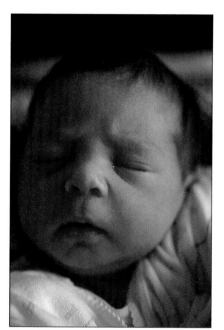

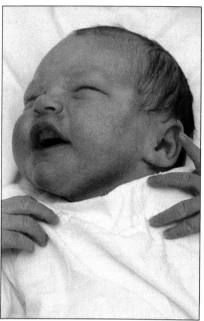

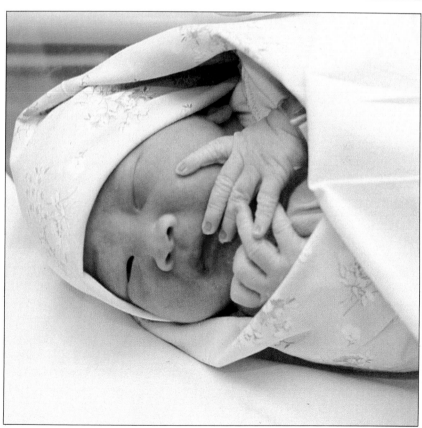

Your baby's genitals may appear red and swollen immediately after birth. If your baby is a boy, the scrotum may seem especially large in relation to the rest of the body. The swelling may be due to hormones you produced during pregnancy, or it may be due to an accumulation of fluid in the sac surrounding the testes. The swelling is harmless and the fluid is gradually absorbed into his body during the first three months of life. In addition, one or both testes may be undescended. ·

If your baby is a girl she may have a vaginal discharge or a little bleeding, and her clitoris may be swollen. This, too, is due to hormones produced by the mother. The discharge usually clears up in a couple of days.

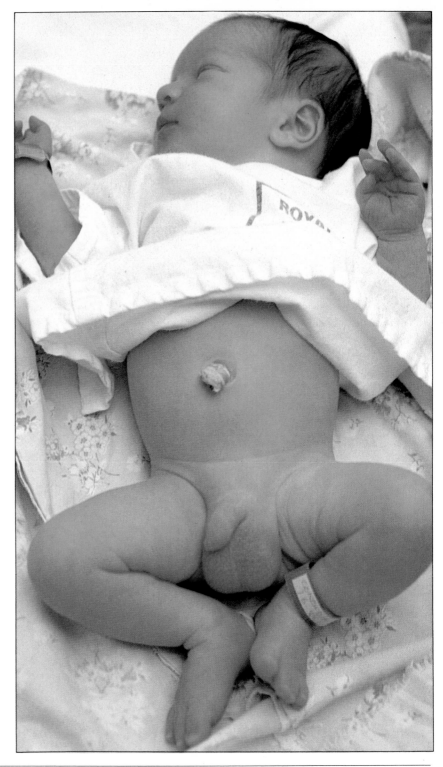

having a high content of red cells which are broken down after birth. One of the end products of this breaking down of red cells is the yellow pigment called bilirubin, which increases in the blood to cause jaundice.

Before birth most of the bilirubin is removed by the placenta and dealt with by the mother's body but after birth the baby has to deal with it alone, and her liver at birth is unable to excrete the bilirubin sufficiently rapidly to prevent the jaundice. This is because a newborn's liver is immature and can't handle the amount of bilirubin which is overloading the blood. It takes a few days for your baby's liver to increase in capacity and deal with the pigment. Physiological jaundice clears by the end of the first week as long as the baby feeds well and does not become dehydrated.

If a more serious type of jaundice occurs within the first few days, and the bilirubin is significantly elevated, this needs to be treated using phototherapy (lights).

Your baby may be born with a wrinkly, dry peeling skin, most noticeable on her soles and palms. This is a temporary condition only and will disappear within a couple of days.

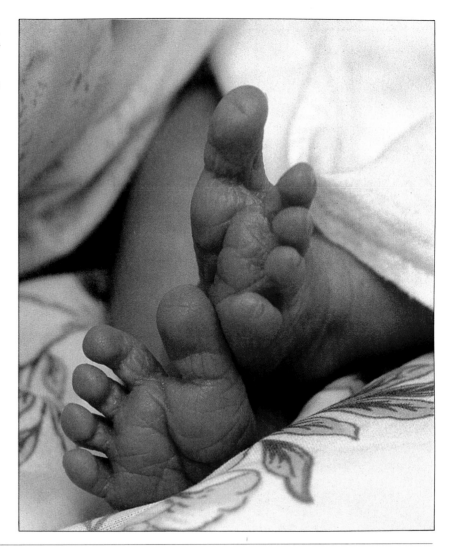

HEAD SHAPE

Your baby's head may appear lopsided, pointed or flattened. This is caused by "molding" of her skull to conform to the confines of the birth canal. The four large plates of the skull are not attached to each other; they can be pushed together by pressure of the birth canal, enabling your baby to fit through this narrow passageway. It can take up to two weeks for a newborn baby's head to assume its normal shape.

Nearly every baby is born with its head out of shape. During the preliminary tests your baby's head will be examined and the degree of molding or distortion noted. Molding is caused by the gentle pressure exerted by the uterus and vaginal walls upon the baby's head as it passes through the pelvis during delivery. The pressure causes the bones of the skull to overlap in such a way that the diameter of the head can be diminished by as much as ½in (1cm), this gives an elongated, abnormal appearance. Molding is a natural phenomenon and your baby's head will begin to return to its normal round shape within 24 to 48 hours of delivery.

Some babies heads are molded more than others and the degree of molding usually varies with the length of the labor. Molding is more noticeable when the labor is long and difficult. Molding does not damage the baby's head or brain. Babies that have been delivered by cesarean section or as breech deliveries generally do not have skull molding; however, the head may be molded if there is a long difficult labor.

You may notice other unusual features about the shape of your baby's head. These include a *caput succedaneum*, a swelling of the scalp caused by pressure of the baby's head on the dilating cervix during the first stage of labor. The caput may be on one side of the head and varies in size according to the duration of labor. A caput is usually normal but may signal obstruction. It is a collection of fluid within the layers of the scalp and gradually disappears in the first 12 to 24 hours.

A cyst-like swelling (*cephalhematoma*) may be present on one side of the baby's head, or very occasionally on both sides. A cephalhematoma is

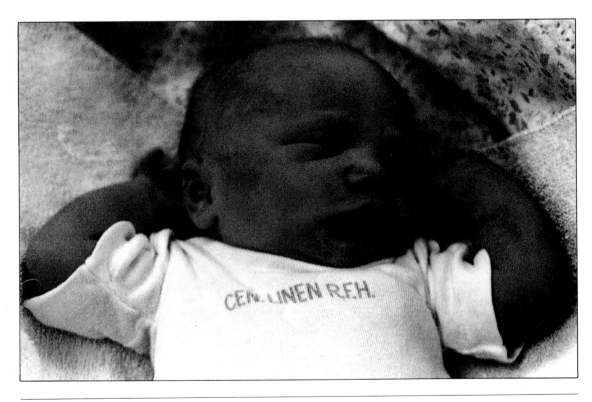

CEN. LINEN R.F.H.

YOUR BABY'S PHYSIOLOGY

Before birth, your baby lives in a wonderfully protected, temperature-controlled and sound-insulated environment, floating in a bath of warm fluid, and with all his physical needs supplied. Oxygen, glucose, vitamins and minerals are provided by way of the umbilical link to the mother, and the baby's carbon dioxide and other waste products are carried off into the mother's blood. But even here your baby is beginning to rehearse for his future life outside the uterus, tentatively expanding his chest and trying out his arm, leg and back muscles.

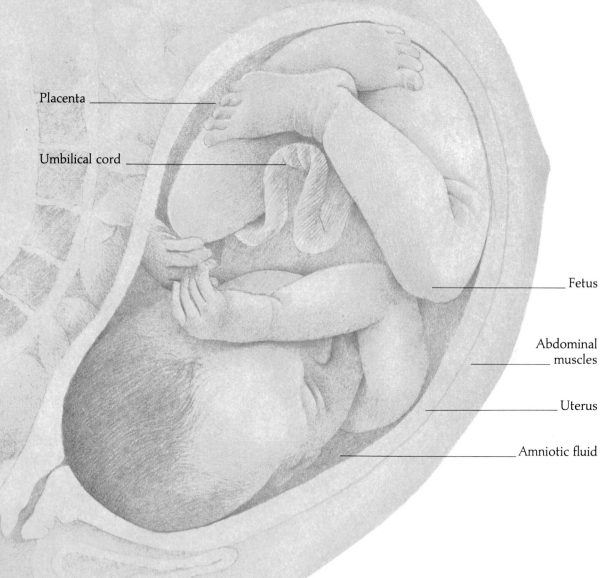

Placenta _____

Umbilical cord _____

_____ Fetus

Abdominal
_____ muscles

_____ Uterus

_____ Amniotic fluid

The transition from life in the uterus to life in the outside world will involve some major changes in the physiology of your baby, to allow independent life. The most radical changes will be in the heart and blood circulation, but your baby must also start to obtain his own oxygen supply through his newly functional lungs, digest his own food, regulate his own heat, and begin to cope with the new barrage of sensory information which will fall upon him.

In the uterus, all nutritional needs are supplied by the placenta in which a baby's blood, while not mixing with her mother's, comes into such intimate contact with it, that oxygen and other supplies can easily diffuse from mother to baby. The blood passing to the placenta carries away the baby's waste products to the mother's blood.

Before birth, your baby's heart must pump blood not only to her own body, but also through the umbilical cord to the large masses of placental vessels.

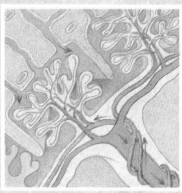

In the placenta there are fifteen to twenty bays of maternal blood in which the tree-like umbilical vessels are immersed. Here the nutrient exchange occurs.

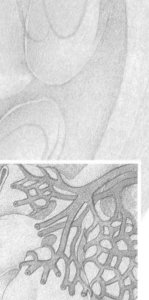

At this stage, your baby's lungs are almost solid and her tiny air sacs are compressed. It will take her some hours of effort before her lungs will be expanded fully.

The blood is no longer being pumped to the placenta; the shunts which largely by-passed the lungs are closed, and a full supply goes to the lungs.

Once she's born, a baby's supply-line to her mother is cut and the newborn child must quickly adapt to her new mode of life. Major changes now occur in her heart and lungs and she must provide her own oxygen supply. She must also process her own food, so there is an increase in the activity of the enzymes in her intestine.

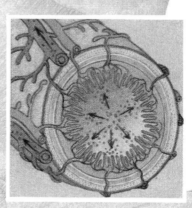

The digestive system has been operating at low level for some time, but now your baby must acquire, digest and absorb all her own nourishment.

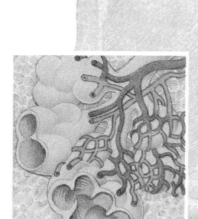

Oxygen lack forces the baby to take a strong inspiration and this expansion of the chest sucks air into the lungs and opens up the vital air sacs.

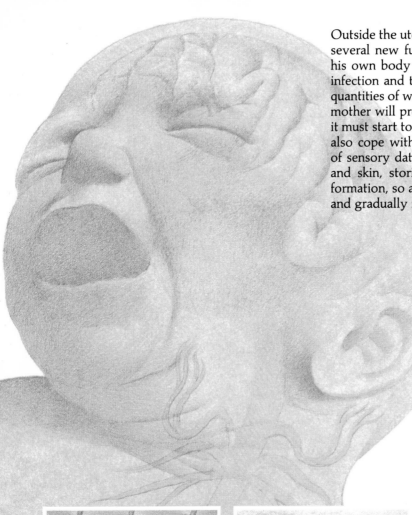

Outside the uterus, your baby must now take on several new functions, including the control of his own body temperature, the defence against infection and the excretion of greatly increased quantities of waste material. Antibodies from the mother will protect it for some weeks, but soon it must start to produce its own. Your baby must also cope with the enormously increased input of sensory data via his ears, eyes, nose, tongue and skin, storing and coordinating all this information, so as to gain knowledge of the world and gradually form his own personality.

Your baby's skin is liberally supplied with nerve endings which send information to his brain about touch, pain, temperature and pressure.

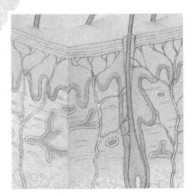

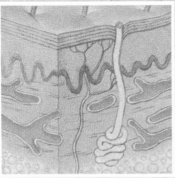

Excess heat can only be lost by the widening of blood vessels near the surface of the skin to radiate heat away. Cooling by sweat evaporation is minimal.

Because babies shiver little, brown fat is important in raising body temperature. It is readily available and is the main source of body heat.

really just a large bruise, formed when a tiny blood vessel has burst, in exactly the same way as when you bruise your skin. You know that bruises go through several color changes and disappear completely and so will your baby's. The cephalhematoma may be fairly large, measuring about $1\frac{1}{2}$in in diameter and about $\frac{1}{4}$in thick. It is nearly always the result of a difficult labor and is caused by the pressure of the baby's head against the posterior part of the mother's pelvis. A cephalhematoma does not require treatment but should be watched to make sure that the swelling reduces in size and the blood within is absorbed. The process may take up to six months, but will leave a perfectly normal head.

HAIR

My granny always used to say that she liked a baby with a good head of hair but quite a few babies are born completely bald. The amount of hair on a baby's body and head varies greatly. Lanugo is the fine downy hair that appeared on your baby around the 36th week of pregnancy and some babies, in addition to a soft down on their heads, may have quite a lot of hair over their shoulders and down their spines at birth. This, however, does not mean they will be hairy as they grow up. Both the presence or lack of hair at birth are normal and any such hair usually falls off quite soon after birth. More permanent hair will follow. The hair on your baby's head at birth may not represent the color she will eventually end up with.

EYES

Most babies are born with blue-gray eyes, or rather the white part of the newborn baby's eye is white, the iris is blue, and the pupil appears black. This is because melanin, the body's natural pigment, is not present in the eyes at birth. Asian and Black babies may have brown eyes at birth.

If your baby is going to have differently-colored eyes the color will gradually develop over a period of weeks or months. Her eyes may not reach their permanent color until she is six months old. Both eyes usually change color simultaneously, but a very few babies end up with different colored eyes and this is also perfectly normal.

Most babies are born with rather puffy eyes as a result of the natural pressure during birth. The swelling usually goes down within a couple of days. There may be patches of red or purple on her eyelids as well. About one-third of babies have epicanthic folds – pleats of skin between the inner ends of the upper and lower lids. The folds commonly disappear as the child grows older.

Hemorrhages occasionally occur in a baby's eyes at birth. These can be seen as small, red, triangle-shaped marks in the white of the eye and are caused by the tiny vessels of the eyes bleeding as a result of pressure on the baby's head during labor and delivery. They can look dramatic but are harmless and disappear spontaneously after a week and require no treatment. They cause no damage to the eye or the baby's sight.

Newborn babies don't achieve simultaneous binocular vision until they are about six weeks old and it may seem at times that your baby looks cross-eyed; don't worry at all. The muscles controlling eye movements are very weak in a newborn baby and they take more than a month to become strong and mature. Gradually, as a baby's eyes begin to focus the muscles line up and become parallel. Don't think that your baby can't focus at all because every baby can, from the first day, but only at a distance of 8–10 inches. So, when you chat to her or play with her fingers, make sure you hold them this close to her face so she will see quite clearly. Your baby starts to recognize your face within the first couple of day of life and this is very important to the bonding process.

You may find that your baby does not shed tears when she cries during the first few weeks. It can take some babies up to four or five months to produce tears.

GENITALS

Both sexes may have genitals that appear large in relation to the baby's size, especially if the infant is premature. Such swelling is due to the presence of the mother's hormones in the baby's bloodstream.

BIRTHMARKS

There is hardly a baby born without a blemish somewhere. I remember on the second day deciding to go over my baby and look at every conceivable place to see if there were any. I found none until I looked at his hairline and there was this little birthmark – a small, enlarged blood vessel. When I pointed it out to the nurses, they called it a stork bite.

Birthmarks (*nevi*) are common in newborn babies and mainly consist simply of an abnormal collection of small blood vessels just underneath the skin. They may be present on any part of your baby and, while the majority of them disappear, some remain and others increase in size. They are quite normal and need no treatment.

Spider birthmarks are relatively small marks that appear shortly after birth as a network or a cobweb of dilated vessels. They generally disappear after the end of the first or second year.

Pigmented nevi are brownish patches occurring anywhere on the body. They are usually pale and nearly always enlarge as the child grows but seldom become any darker.

Salmon patches, also called stork's marks, are pink marks often seen above the bridge of the nose, on the eyelids, and over the nape of the neck just below the hairline. These are mild discolorations of the skin and they usually fade with time, often within a few days.

Port wine stains are bright red or even purple marks found anywhere on the body, frequently on the face and neck. They may occasionally be quite extensive and the skin is usually of a different texture with the marks having sharply-defined edges. Port wine stains are dilated capillaries in the skin and they are permanent; these days they are very successfully treated with laser treatments and the skin can be made almost perfect by using camouflage make-up, specially manufactured for this purpose.

Strawberry marks appear first as tiny red dots and are not always obvious. They are the result of dilated blood vessels. They may grow alarmingly during the early months of life, becoming red raised lumps, but then begin to shrivel during the baby's second year, and eventually disappear without leaving a scar.

Blue marks (also called Mongolian blue spots), which look like bruises, often occur on the lower backs of babies with dark skin tones (nearly all Black and Asian babies, and some Mediterranean babies, have them). They are completely harmless and fade away naturally.

The natural pigmentation of dark-skinned babies may not appear for several hours or days after birth. Dark-skinned babies often have Mongolian blue spots, harmless dark bluish-black discolorations of the skin. These spots usually appear on the backs and/or buttocks, and occur in almost all black and Asian babies. The spots, which look like bruises, fade away naturally.

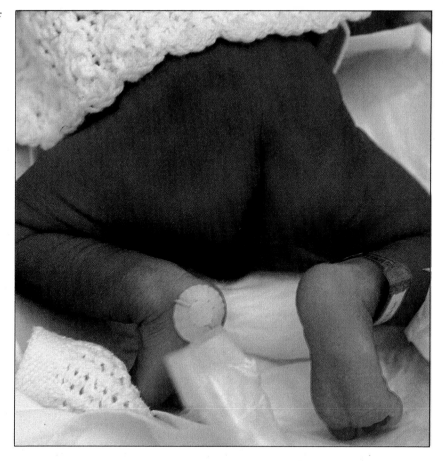

SPOTS AND RASHES

A baby's skin is like an unstable thermometer with the mercury shooting up and down and can change color from pink to blue and back again. You will see red blotches, while blotches and the legs may be a different color from the rest of the body. In the first few weeks of life don't worry about these changes, your baby's skin is simply becoming mature.

Newborn babies often have spots and rashes that are generally harmless. Most of these occur because it takes several months for your baby's skin to stabilize.

Milia are small white spots that appear mainly on the bridge of the nose, but also elsewhere on the face. They are caused by the temporary blockage of the sebaceous glands that secrete sebum to lubricate the skin. Milia are very common and require no treatment. You should never squeeze them. They nearly always disappear within a few weeks.

Heat rash is the name given to small red spots that often appear, especially on a baby's face and, if you look closely, they are related to individual sweat glands. They can occur when a baby is overwrapped and sweaty, but also develop in babies who are not overheated, and in cool weather. Apart from trying to keep the baby's clothes and blankets appropriate to the room temperature, there is no special treatment. It is best to accept the fact that most normal babies go through spotty phases (particularly as you begin to introduce each new food later on).

White spots may be seen on the roof of the mouth. They are called Epstein's pearls and are harmless cysts, not to be mistaken for thrush or Koplik spots, which are used to diagnose measles.

Urticaria is nettle rash. There is usually a raised white center, surrounded by a red flare in the skin. It is quite common for nettle rash to appear during the first week of life but, unlike any other rash, it usually disappears within 10 to 20 minutes while other ones continue to form. Urticaria is caused by a hypersensitivity to an outside stimulus. There is no need for treatment and it does not recur after the first month or so.

SPECIAL CARE BABIES

PREMATURITY

The medical definition of a premature baby is one that is born prior to 38 weeks gestational period.

An infant that is born at 40 weeks, weighing less than the 10th percentage for weight, is considered to be growth retarded, not premature.

A small but mature baby stands a much better chance of surviving than does a large baby delivered unduly early.

The main causes of prematurity are not completely understood, and in a large majority of cases the cause is unknown. Various factors are associated with premature labor and delivery, including multiple pregnancy, maternal disease and malnutrition.

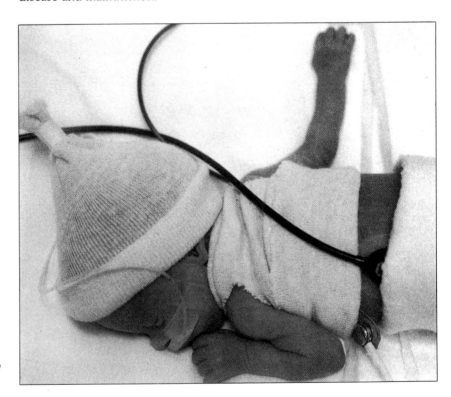

Babies that are premature (less than 38 weeks of gestation) will usually be put in an incubator and need special care.

Premature babies have difficulty regulating their body temperatures and so must be kept warm. The incubator helps keep their temperatures steady. They also may have breathing difficulties as their respiratory systems are immature, and may need to be monitored constantly.

A premature baby's skin is red, wrinkled and covered with soft hair. Her head is small but appears large in proportion to her body and her skull bones are soft. Her eyes stay closed, her sucking reflex is poor, and she sleeps more or less continuously. She may have respiratory difficulties and a poorly developed temperature control.

Respiratory difficulty is due to her lungs being immature. She will probably have shallow, irregular, rapid breathing, and may develop a condition called respiratory distress syndrome, which sometimes requires the use of a ventilator. Since the baby chills easily due to her poorly developed heat-regulating mechanism, she may be placed in an incubator to maintain a uniform body temperature.

A premature baby is also more susceptible to infection because her resistance is poor. Breastfeeding plays an important part in building resistance and protecting your baby, therefore breast milk is particularly beneficial to a premature baby.

Jaundice appearing anytime during the first week or two of life is fairly common in premature babies, as it is in normal weight ones (see page 16). The baby will be frequently examined so that the jaundice can be treated if it becomes too severe.

Anemia, or iron deficiency, may develop in premature babies or those of low birth weight. Because the small baby grows more rapidly in proportion to her birth weight than does the large baby, she exhausts her more-than-adequate store of iron reserves quite quickly, and is then liable to develop iron deficiency anemia. To prevent this, premature babies are given iron by mouth from the age of about four weeks.

Premature babies are usually put in thermostatically controlled incubators to maintain body temperature. Oxygen may be administered. The baby, in ideal circumstances can be nursed without clothes. Infections can be avoided by isolation; to a certain extent, this is achieved by the incubator itself. While a premature baby is handled as little as possible, parents are given free access to the baby (although consult the nursing staff as to what you can actually do) so that bonding to the baby by both parents and vice versa is accelerated. The baby is not usually bathed until her condition is satisfactory.

Feeding is usually a problem with premature babies, since they often lose quite a lot of weight in the first week. It is important that premature babies begin feeding as soon as possible, and that they maintain a high intake of protein and carbohydrate during the first weeks. The method of feeding depends on the baby's condition. If she is very small and feeble, she may be fed small amounts every two or three hours by means of a special fine tube passed down her throat into her stomach. The tube causes the baby no discomfort. Larger premature babies may be able to suck from a special bottle with a soft nipple, and babies over 4lb 8oz can usually feed from the breast. Small feeds are given regularly during the first week or two of life and the amount is then increased gradually. The smaller the baby, the more often she needs feeding in order to maintain body temperature. Just think of a tiny humming bird; it never stops feeding during 24 hours because its weight is so low it needs constant food to stoke up the metabolic burners and keep the temperature normal.

Bonding is especially important for the premature baby in an incubator. In ideal situations, you will see your baby at the earliest opportunity and handle her as soon as her condition allows. Separation is minimized, though any is certain to cause you some distress.

The premature baby almost always develops normally and, in most cases, after the first few weeks no one would know your baby was born prematurely. How long she needs to be kept in an incubator varies according to her maturity and birth weight, though usually she will be kept in the hospital until she reaches 5lb.

LOW-BIRTH-WEIGHT BABIES

Your baby may be of a low birth weight but otherwise well developed. This is often due to growth retardation during pregnancy caused by a number of factors, some of which include your health and nutrition, your own size, if you smoked, and if you've had twins or triplets, or if there were fetal infections or malformations. Similar to a premature baby, yours will appear thin and scrawny, have little fat on her body, have cracked skin and poor temperature control. Your low-birth-weight baby will need special care in the hospital, and may be kept in an incubator. She needs more calories than normal weight babies, and may be fed frequently.

SPECIAL CARE BABIES

Some babies need special care in the hospital, most often because they are premature, of low birth weight or have jaundice. Some can be cared for on the postnatal ward, while others will go in an incubator in the Special Care Baby Unit. If yours is a special care baby, it is important for you to be with her as much as possible. There will be lots of machinery and apparatus, and you should ask the nurse to explain what is happening to your baby. If your baby does not have feeding problems, you will be able to feed as normal. Very small premature babies cannot suck properly at first and will need to be fed by tube. You can express your breast milk to be fed to your baby in this way. Then, later on, you can breastfeed normally when the baby is mature enough.

INJURIES AT BIRTH

Major birth injuries are very rare indeed. The process of birth may cause a few minor injuries, especially if the delivery has been long and difficult, but the worst ones are usually avoided by resorting to cesarean section. None of the following birth injuries are serious. Cephalhematoma is a bruise on the head that develops as a result of bleeding from one of the blood vessels beneath the tissue covering the bone. This swelling disappears after some weeks, although the edge may be felt for months. It does not require any treatment but must be watched closely for enlargements.

Scalp bruises which occur under the scalp and can spread anywhere across the baby's head, disappear after a couple of weeks. Forcep bruises are the result of a forceps delivery. They usually appear on the baby's cheeks and quickly fade. If your baby has been delivered by vacuum extractor she may have bruising where the suction cup was applied.

Small incised wounds of the presenting part — usually the head but occasionally the buttocks — may be caused by artificial rupture of the membranes, internal fetal scalp electrode used to monitor fetal heartbeat during labor, or blood being taken from the baby before birth.

OPPOSITE
Twins are often smaller than single-delivery babies and may need special care for a few days. They will usually be put into incubators, which help to regulate their temperatures.

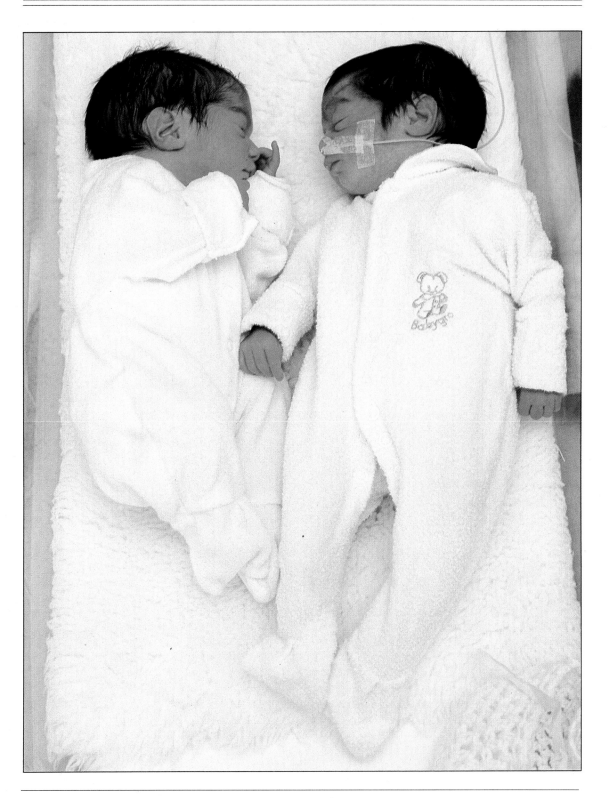

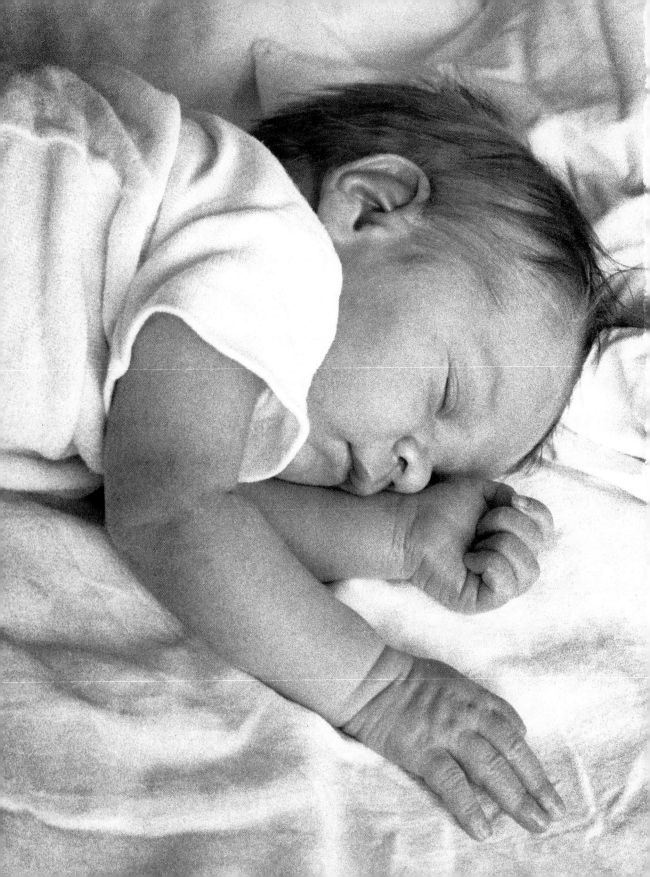

2

YOUR BABY'S BEHAVIOR

Your newborn baby is much more interesting than you may think. From birth, babies present different personalities; some are placid and "well-behaved," others are more demanding. Study your baby, get to know him, discover his idiosyncrasies and eccentricities. Some of his behavior may frighten you a little at first unless you are prepared for it: changing skin color, rapid jerky movements, an irregular breathing pattern and snuffles may give you a shock unless you know why it is that a baby behaves the way he does.

Your newborn baby is born with a number of abilities, only some of which are reflexes designed for his protection. He can see, hear, suck, swallow, smell, taste, yawn, hiccup, sneeze, cough, stretch, salivate, sleep, excrete, and cry. Within a few days of birth he can recognize you by your smell and soon after that by sight. Your baby's perceptive abilities are much greater than his motor skills. In other words, he can see, hear, understand, relate to you and other people more easily than he can control the movements of his body.

HICCUPS, SNEEZING, SNUFFLES

Newborn babies hiccup quite a lot. Hiccuping is normal, so don't let it worry you. Hiccups are caused by sudden, irregular contractions of the primitive diaphragm which hasn't quite got breathing in and breathing out into a steady rhythm. They are a sign that the muscles involved in respiration between the ribs, the diaphragm, and the abdomen, are getting stronger and trying to work in harmony. Babies don't seem to mind hiccoughs, so you should just ignore them.

Babies are sensitive to bright lights and sometimes sneeze whenever they open their eyes for the first few days. This is because light stimulates the nerves to the nose as well as to the eyes. Even if your baby is sneezing a lot it doesn't necessarily mean that he has a cold. The lining of a baby's nose is sensitive, and sneezing is essential to clear out the nasal passages and prevent dust from getting down into the lungs. Fits of sneezing are quite common in young babies.

Some babies make a snuffling noise through their noses when they are breathing. It may sound as if your baby has a cold, and his nose may even run a bit with clear fluid. This is partly because breathing through his nose is new to him, and partly because he has small nasal passages. As he gets older, and his nose gets larger, the snuffling will stop. No treatment for snuffles is needed unless feeding is affected by his breathing difficulty, in which case you must contact your doctor.

Sneezing is a common response in newborns. They have very small noses and nasal passages that can be irritated easily.

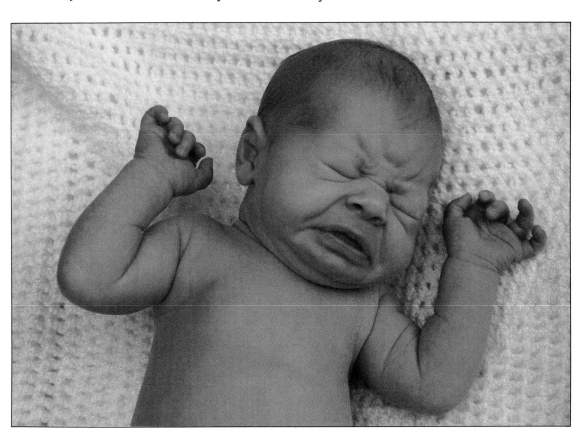

Babies exhibit certain behavior right from birth. If your baby is turned to one side quickly, his eyes will turn in the opposite direction and will then slowly move in the direction in which they have been turned.

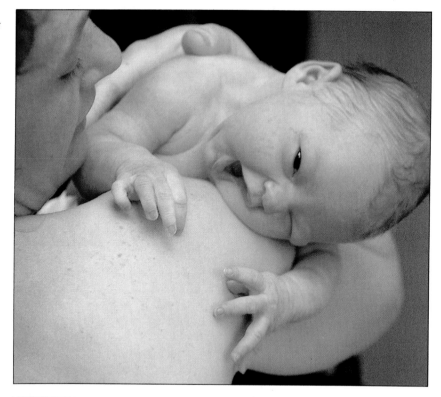

Quiet, watchful behavior need not be sex-determined. It is no more appropriate to expect a girl to be inactive than it is to believe that boys by nature are more demonstrative and demanding.

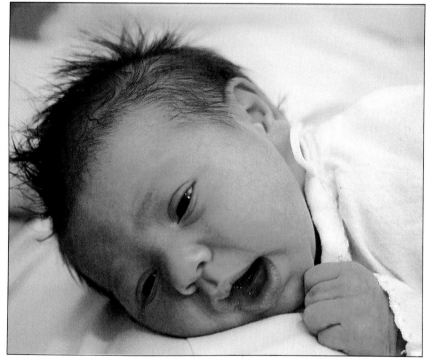

SPITTING UP AFTER FEEDING

All babies bring up milk but some do it more than others. Highly active, very alert babies who exhibit rapid movements of the arms and legs are most likely to do it frequently – especially in the first few weeks. Some milk wells out of the mouth of most babies after a feed. Less food will be lost if you keep your baby upright and don't lie him down flat.

BREATHING

Once a baby is breathing satisfactorily after his delivery he continues to breathe fairly regularly at the rate of about 40 breaths per minute for the first one or two days. The rate of breathing then falls to about 25 breaths per minute when he is a few months old. His breathing won't necessarily be even and smooth though, throughout each 24-hour day. Your newborn baby has small lungs and his breathing will seem shallow when compared to an adult's. You may notice that his abdomen moves quite a lot. This is because your baby's lungs are smaller proportionally to his size. When your baby is asleep, he may breathe quite deeply and quickly for a few seconds, then breathe slowly and almost stop altogether. This is quite normal; don't be frightened if at first you cannot detect your baby's breathing. It will become stronger and more regular as he gets older.

All babies make strange sounds when they breathe. Sometimes the breathing is fast and noisy, while at other times it may be irregular. Your baby may snuffle with each breath in and out because the bridge of his nose is low, and air is trying to get through the very small nasal passages. Premature babies' breathing is marked by irregularity and periods when the breathing seems to be very fast and then quite a frightening period when the baby's breathing slows down to almost nothing and you think he is

You may also find that your baby yawns, and these yawns can be accompanied by various noises. Babies also sniffle, grunt and snort; many newborns snore when they sleep. This is because their nasal passages are so small. These noises often vanish as the baby's nose and sinuses enlarge.

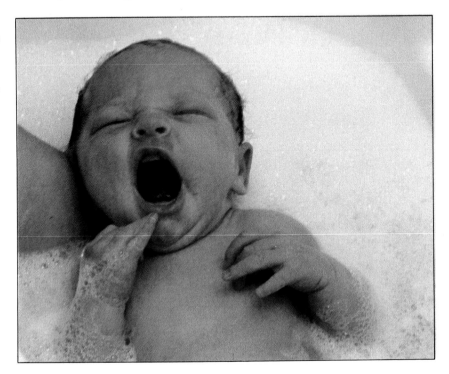

going to stop. After a few seconds he will suddenly start breathing quite fast again, this is perfectly normal.

If, however, your baby's breathing becomes labored with a rate increasing to 60 or more breaths per minute and his chest is drawn sharply in with each breath, contact your doctor immediately.

POSTURE AND POSITION

Your new baby will have certain postures typical to him because of his physical immaturity. When your baby is placed on his back, his head will touch the mattress. He will probably turn his head towards one side, extend the arm on that side and flex the opposite arm in towards his chest.

If your baby is placed on his stomach, he will again turn his head towards a preferred side, and probably position himself with his arms and legs flexed under him and his bottom in the air. This posture vanishes when he is a few weeks old.

All of the postures of your newborn baby when not lying down are dominated by his gradually acquired ability to manage and control his head. After birth the head is literally too heavy for the muscles of his back and neck.

By one week old if your baby is comfortably held against your shoulder, he will lift his head away in little intermittent jerks.

By three weeks he will be able to hold his head clear of the shoulder for several seconds at a time.

By six weeks most babies will be able to support their heads for a minute or two.

REFLEXES

All newborn babies have reflexes which are instinctive movements designed to protect them. They last until voluntary movements on your baby's part take their place, generally around three months. Voluntary movements, which your baby decides to make for himself, are purposeful and have an aim in view. Two of the easiest to elicit are those to protect the

Premature or low-birth-weight babies may sleep more than full-term or more mature babies. Often, they will be less active than mature babies. If your baby is getting special care, do not worry if he seems less active than a full-term one; he will still kick and move just like other babies, although it may be with less force and strength.

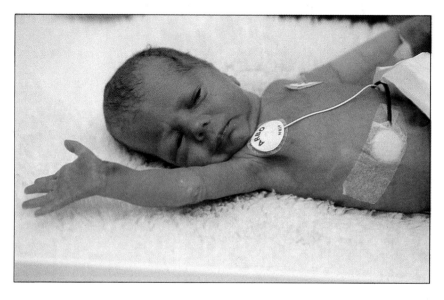

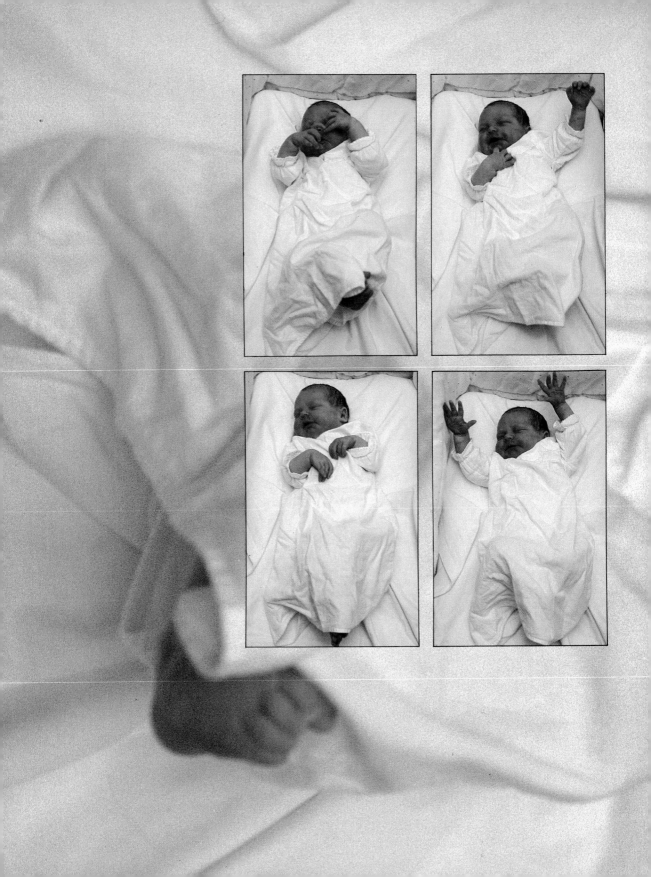

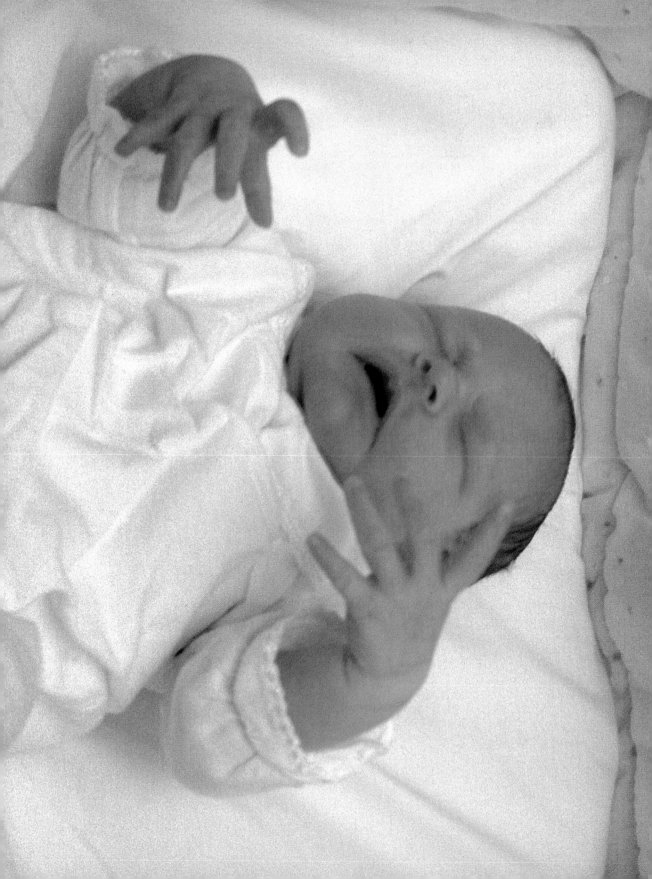

Newborn babies are surprisingly active. Their movements are normally jerky and twitching, especially if they are premature. The more mature the baby is at birth, the smoother his movements are.

Some babies move much more than others do, constantly wriggling and stretching their limbs. Others are content to lie quietly, rarely moving around. Babies especially like to stretch out their legs, kicking them around. This kicking movement helps to strengthen their muscles and joints.

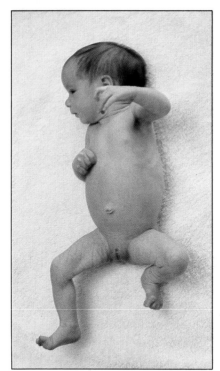

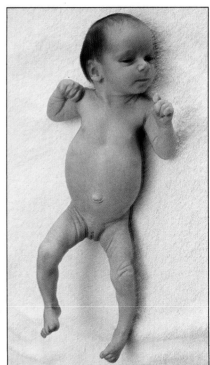

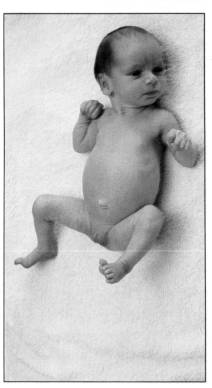

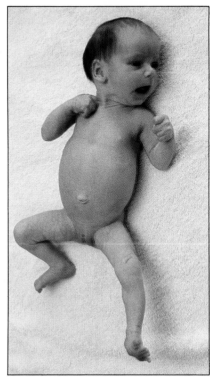

eyes and to maintain breathing. For example, if you touch your newborn baby's eyelids he will close them tightly, and if you lightly hold his nose between your finger and thumb he will try to remove them by striking out with his hands.

During the examination of your baby in the first 24–36 hours after birth the doctor may test for the following reflex responses:

● The rooting reflex. Your baby makes this rooting movement when he is searching for your breast to start feeding. If you gently stroke your baby's cheek you will find that he turns his head in the direction of the finger and opens his mouth.

● The grasp reflex will be demonstrated when pressure is applied to the palm of a baby's hand and he automatically clenches his fist. In the majority of babies this reflex is so powerful they can be lifted by their fingers if an adult's thumbs are pressed gently into the palms. This derives from our ancient ancestors who were tree-dwellers and newborn babies had to cling to their mothers' backs. For this reason, they had a very strong grasp reflex in order to hang on; their feet could grasp, too. In other words, the hands and the feet were "prehensile". This reflex is generally lost around three months old. If you touch the soles of your baby's feet you will also notice that his toes curl downwards as if to grip something.

● The walking reflex involves a newborn baby moving his legs in a walking or stepping action if he is held upright underneath the arms and his feet allowed to touch a firm surface. This is not the reflex that encourages a baby to stand upright and walk; the skill of standing and walking has to be completely relearned when the muscles and joints of the body, and the baby's sense of balance, is much more mature around 12 months.

● Your baby will assume what appears to be a crawling position if placed on his stomach. This is because his legs are still curled up toward his body as they were in the womb. When he kicks his legs he may be able to shuffle in a vague crawling manner and actually move in his crib slightly. This reflex will disappear as soon as his legs uncurl and he lies flat.

● The Moro reflex is used as a test of a baby's general condition and the normality of his central nervous system. During this test your baby is undressed and held at an angle, the back of his head being supported by the examiner's hand. The baby's head is then allowed to suddenly drop back a little and this causes him to immediately throw out his legs and arms with his fingers extended. Then slowly he draws his arms into his body with his fingers clenched and his knees bent up to his abdomen. Both sides of his body should respond simultaneously and equally. The same response, known as the "startle" reflex, occurs if your baby is disturbed by any sudden loud noise or violent movement.

Additionally, all babies have the following capabilities:

● Every baby is born with the reflex to suck. The sucking reflex is when pressure in the baby's mouth, on the palate just inside the upper margin of the gum, provokes quite strong and rapid sucking which continues for some time. A baby doesn't suck so much as chomp. The nipple and the areola should be placed well back in the baby's mouth so that the chomping movements exert a negative pressure which is extremely strong and very efficient at sucking out milk, but also can cause sore nipples if the breast

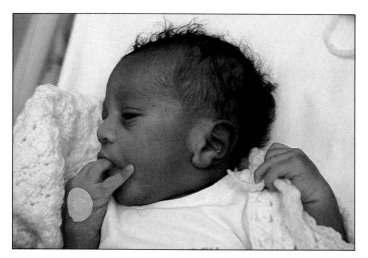

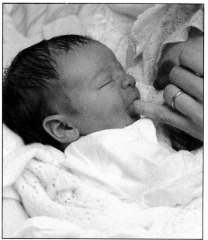

ABOVE
One of the many reflexes your baby will have is the ability to suck, which ensures he will be able to feed. You may find that your baby sucks on his own fingers, or yours if you put them near his mouth. He will turn automatically towards a nipple if it is brushed against one of his cheeks.

RIGHT
Another reflex your baby will have is the ability to grasp. Your new baby will be able to grasp things (like a finger or pencil) quite tightly with either his hands or his feet. This automatic response will be lost within a few months.

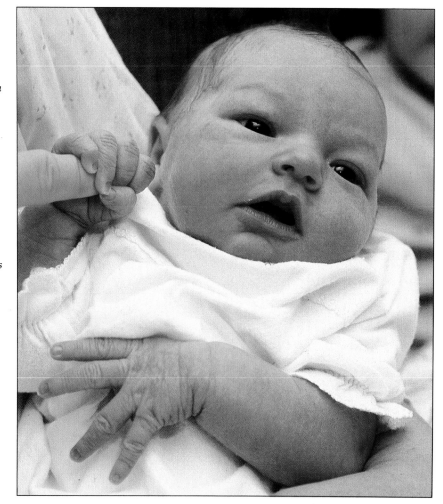

Your baby will have a personality all his own, even when he is sleeping. Some babies are very restless and active, while others sleep calmly and quietly. Most babies need a little help to sleep and all find comfort in being in close physical contact — a mother is ideal. Sucking helps to relieve tension and often prevents a sleeping baby from waking up if he is disturbed. A newborn that is firmly swaddled is not disturbed by any jerky movements.

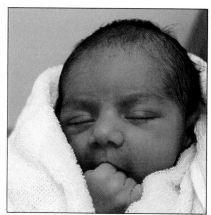
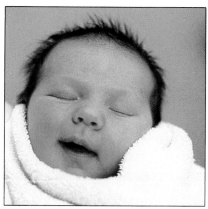
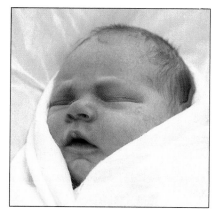

isn't far enough back. This strong negative pressure creates a vacuum into which air will rush and can be inadvertently sucked down into the stomach. This causes gas.

● The swallowing reflex is present in all babies the instant they are born so that they can swallow colostrum or milk straight away.

● The gagging reflex comes into play immediately when too much liquid is taken in. Mucus can also be spat up to clear breathing passages.

SLEEPING

A full-term newborn baby will spend most of his time asleep. The amount of time newborns spend sleeping differs from baby to baby, but the average is about 60 per cent of the day. Don't expect your baby to sleep all the time and don't get worried when he doesn't. Some babies are naturally more wakeful than others.

Your baby will probably fall asleep straight after a feed. If he is tired from feeding and content with a full stomach, he may even drift off near the end of a feed. Your baby will probably sleep very soundly and deeply, and will not be easily woken. It is quite common for your baby to grunt a little during sleep. He will get used to household noises such as banging doors, the vacuum cleaner, television, and the radio. Only sudden noises (or bright lights) will frighten and may wake your baby.

In the beginning babies sleep about 14–18 hours a day. In fact, your baby may spend most of his time between feeds asleep. When you put your baby to sleep, it is usually advisable to lay him on his side rather than on his back. This way if he regurgitates any food he will not inhale it.

If you think your baby is uncomfortable, change his position. He will soon let you know the position he prefers. When you are laying him down, place him with his head touching or close to the top of the crib. This helps to make him feel secure.

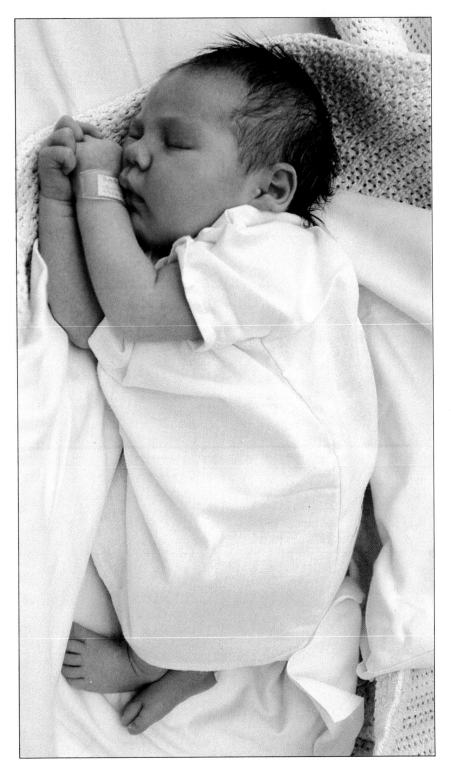

BABY SERGIO

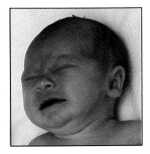

Born: 1 day after his expected date of delivery

Weight: 9lb 1oz (4100g)

Condition: heart rate a bit low before birth, fine almost immediately after

Mother's labor: extremely long, lasting 24 hours

Feeding: breast fed

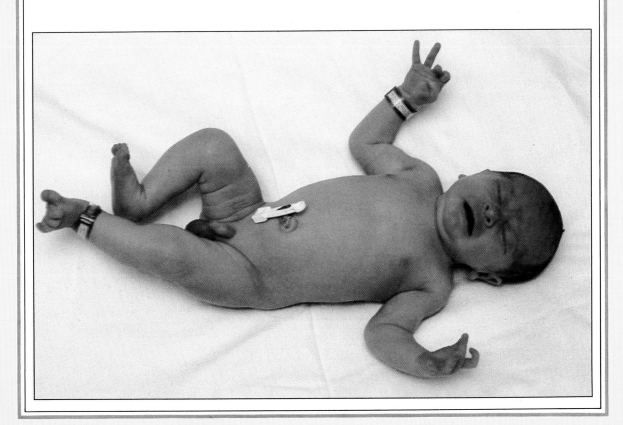

THE FIRST DAY

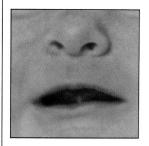

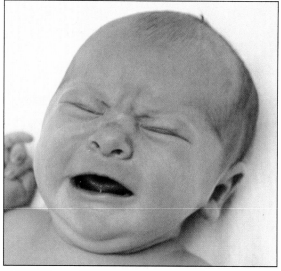

"He had been squashed up inside quite a long time so his eyes were bloodshot and his face was quite red. He had lots of little bright red veins on his face".

"He was very alert right from the beginning and very strong. He used to creep up along my body when I held him and he even turned over while in the hospital. He had this habit of appearing asleep and then one eye would open as if he was checking that everything was OK".

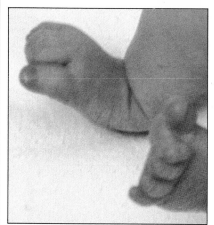

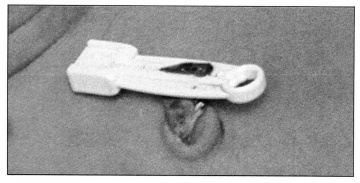

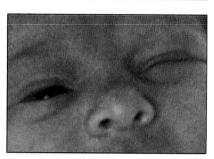

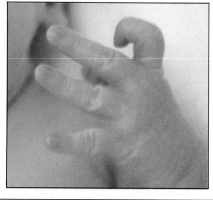

"He came shooting out of the birth canal. His legs were curled up very tight into his body. The doctor said 'Congratulations; you have a girl'. But I had seen his scrotum just visible under his bottom as he was delivered".

THE TENTH DAY

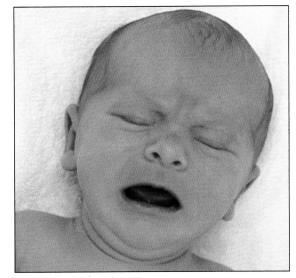

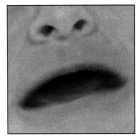

"I found it hard to establish breastfeeding. I got lots of conflicting advice in the hospital. Because of this he lost a lot of weight and only regained his original birth weight when he was 3 weeks old".

"His fingers were quite straight and stretched out right from the beginning. I expected him to be more curled up with clenched fists".

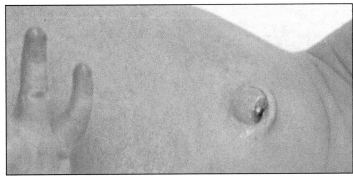

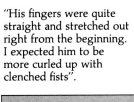

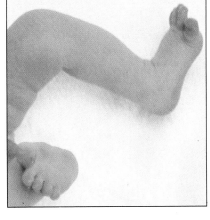

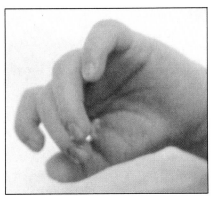

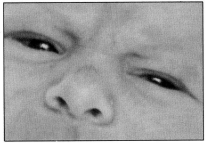

"He cried more often after we came home. I thought he might have been picking up my feelings of insecurity. However, he soon settled down and even began sleeping through the night after he was two weeks old. I'm amazed at how he enjoys activity and being with us. At about a month he seemed to know both of us, turning whenever he heard our voices".

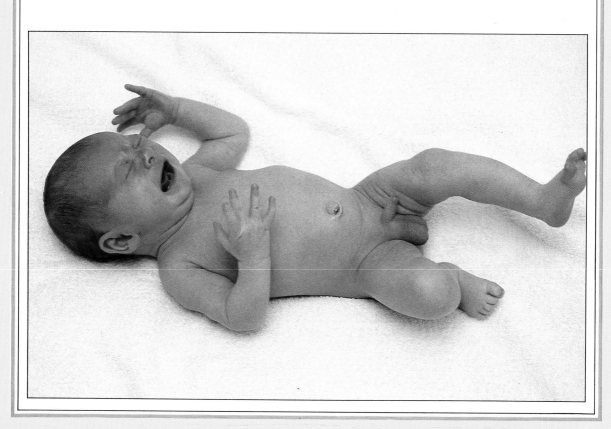

ALERTNESS – SEEING AND HEARING

A newborn baby can see, focus and follow with his eyes, but only at a distance of 8–10 inches from his face. He can differentiate light from dark, and can appreciate the color and shape of a face or a brightly colored object placed about 9 inches away. He responds to bright lights shone in the eyes, but this should only be done by the pediatrician when testing. He can turn his head to follow a human face. By two weeks he can distinguish and prefer your face to others. He may also be able to imitate you if you stick out your tongue.

This is the beginning of socializing; it's your baby's first signs of wanting to be friendly, it's his first conversation. Place your head 8–10 inches away from him and talk, smile, put out your tongue, make lots of dramatic movements with your face so that he can see you and realize that you will respond. In fact, in early conversations, babies call the shots because anxious moms and dads will do anything to make them repeat their movements and expressions.

Newborn babies can hear and respond to sudden noises such as clapping. They do not like sudden loud noises. A sudden loud noise will startle a baby, and his head may jerk back and his arms extend briefly. Quieter sounds and noises make the baby alert and his eyes may open wide and his breathing pattern change. Sometimes his response may simply be a blinking of the eyes. Immediately after birth he can turn to the human voice. He shows more interest in human speech than in other sounds.

The general consensus of opinion states that babies respond more easily

Even at this early age your baby can distinguish between light and dark, see movement and the colors of objects held near to him. Within about two weeks he will be able to recognize your face.

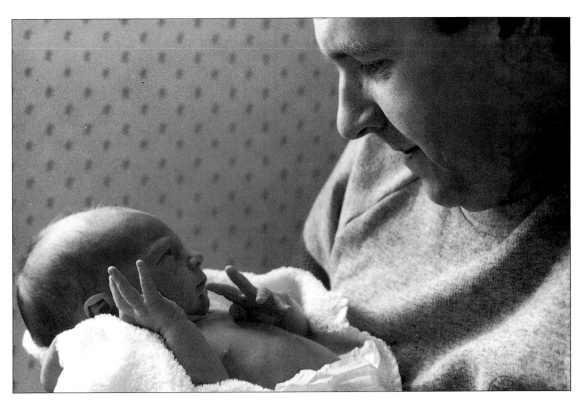

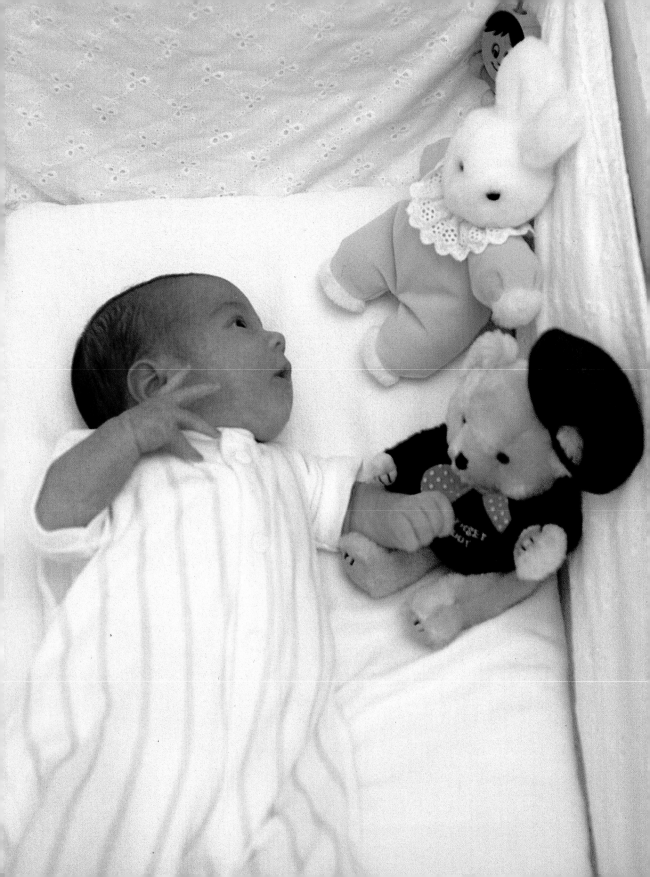

Twins find comfort in being put together. They have just spent nine months together in your uterus and are used to having constant physical closeness and sensation.

Although babies have a number of facial expressions, it may be difficult to interpret what they mean. Babies often grimace or frown but this is not an indication they are unhappy or angry. This baby may be trying to focus his eyes on the people and activities around him, or it may be he is unhappy about the bright lights in his eyes.

OPPOSITE
Many babies are very alert and seem to notice everything that goes on around them. Put toys, mobiles and posters in the crib or room where your baby can see them. This will give him something to focus on.

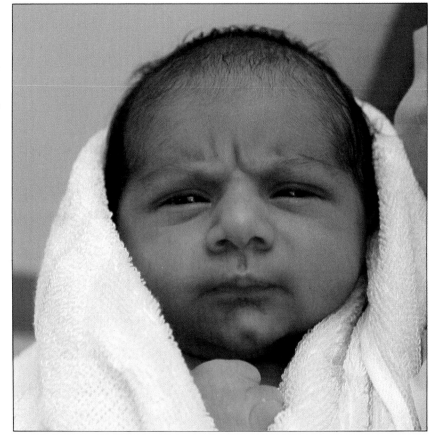

and quickly to higher-pitched female voices. This is quite logical because you'd expect them to respond to their mothers' voices. It's also, of course, why women automatically go into high-pitched baby talk. They seem to know instinctively that this is what the baby responds to best, so don't think that baby talk is useless or silly. It's very important in your baby's development.

COMMUNI-CATION

Newborns communicate chiefly by crying – or the lack of it. The first signs of pleasure shown by your newborn will be when he quietens after being cuddled or upon being placed in a warm bath. He will splay out his toes and flex and extend them.

There is a very old-fashioned and outdated idea that a baby doesn't smile until he's about six weeks old. My mother used to say "it's only gas," but we know now that it certainly isn't. A baby can smile from the moment he's born if he's pleased. When my son, Edmund, was born and laid on my chest, I immediately started to coo "Edmund" at him; his eyes darted towards my face and the direction of the sound, and no one could convince me that he didn't smile. And he smiled from that moment onwards. Babies also communicate by watching and by generalized movements of the body – welcoming gestures.

CRYING

Your baby may make his first cry a few seconds or a few minutes after birth. Some babies cry as soon as their chests are delivered whereas others take several minutes and only cry after normal breathing has been established. The doctor will recognize different types of cry, the characteristics of which may vary according to the maturity and general condition of the baby. The first cry of some babies is more in the nature of a whimper which, after being repeated several times, gradually assumes the full force of a normal cry. Others babies will cough and splutter for a few seconds, or even a few minutes, before they cry normally.

Don't worry if your baby becomes tense, angry and red in the face when crying; this is a normal process. Your baby will take in a big breath, after

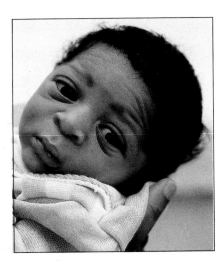

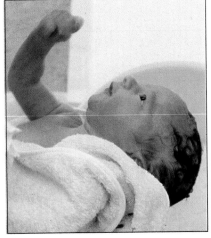

Newborns are aware of many things in their environments. They respond to different tastes, odors and sounds. They react to differences in temperature and restrictions to their breathing.

Babies cry for a number of reasons. They may be unhappy because they are wet, lonely, hungry or tired. Babies do not like being undressed, so yours may cry when you dress or change him. Some babies cry more than others but this is not an indication that your baby is ill or there is anything wrong. Your baby may just be fussy and fretful.

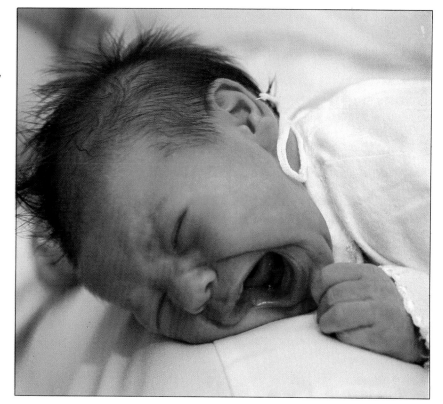

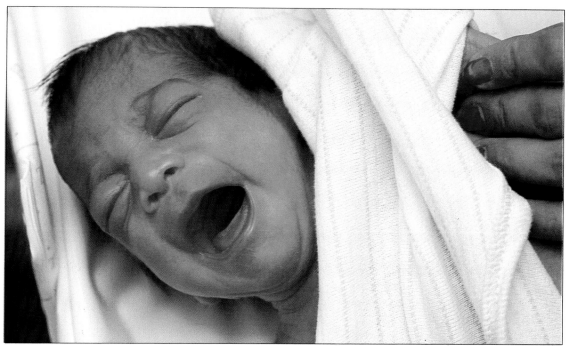

You should not leave your baby to cry. When he does, pick him up and hold him; it may simply be that he is lonely. Or, more rarely, a soiled diaper may be the cause of his distress and he needs changing. His crying may be an indication that he is hungry and ready for a feed.

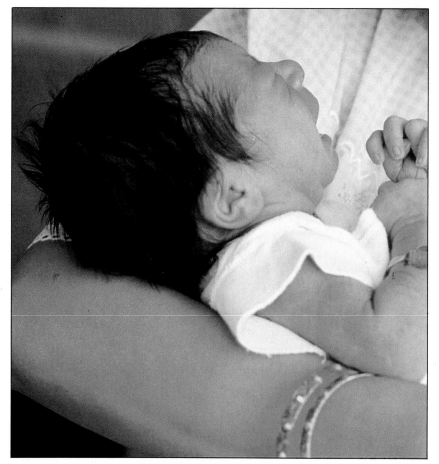

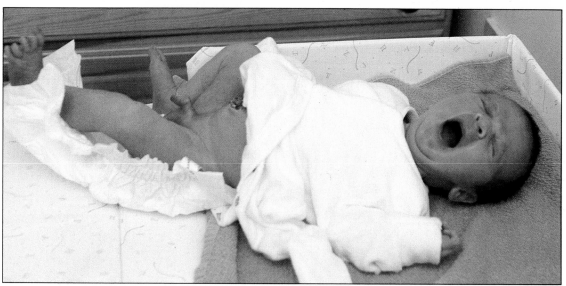

A baby has only one way to communicate his needs. While the cause is often apparent, other, harder to perceive, factors may prompt his reaction. It will take time for you to recognize his different cries and respond appropriately, but it is important that you do respond. The basic foundations of love and security depend on a newborn knowing that his needs will be met.

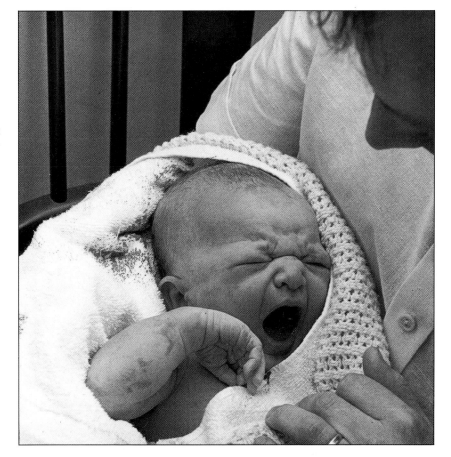

which his whole body will tense, his face will grimace and become bright red, he will open his mouth wide and literally scream. This vigorous type of crying indicates a completely healthy baby and it ensures that normal changes have taken place in his circulation which are essential for his existence in the outside world. It also completes the full expansion of the lungs, ensures that his breathing will be normal, and diminishes the chances of breathing difficulties or infection later on.

Crying is part of a normal baby's life because it's his only way of communicating with you. It is good exercise and causes no harm. The most common causes are discomfort and loneliness. Opinions vary as to how long you should leave a baby to cry; for myself I wanted my baby to grow up knowing that when he asked for attention, he got it, so I never allowed my babies to cry at all; in their first year of life I always went to them and didn't, as my mother advised me, wait and see if they would stop. I felt that if I did this they would grow up thinking that their cries were unimportant, and I wasn't sensitive to them. This is the last thing I wanted my baby to think about me.

1. Hunger is the chief discomfort. On a self-demand schedule, this can be readily appeased if the feed is adequate. But even in the newborn

period, personality is evident. Some babies cry more than others. Some cry louder than others. Some babies may be more tolerant of hunger, others get hungry sooner and demand feeding. Some babies need longer to suck, not to feed just to suck, than others and will cry because they are removed from the breast too soon. However research has shown that most babies take in 80 per cent of their food in under five minutes so your baby will be quite well fed if he spends six or seven minutes on each breast. Don't forget, however, that your baby may be a "sucky baby" – I had two. They liked to suck on the breast and play with it. If your breasts aren't tender and sore, let your baby do this for a little while. Some babies, however, need more milk for their hunger and thirst to be satiated.

2. Another cause of discomfort is too much clothing. It is only when a baby gets somewhat older that a wet or soiled diaper becomes unpleasant and this usually turns out to be a fastidious baby who grows up to become a fastidious child. The belief that an unpleasant smell or taste, such as from vomit, can upset a child is not proven. This largely stems from adults imposing their own tastes on very young babies.

3. Many babies cry when they are tired.

4. Quite often their crying is a reaction to your mood.

5. A common cause of crying is loneliness. Babies love being cuddled and want physical contact almost more than anything else. An experiment done with baby monkeys showed that they preferred a soft, cuddly, imitation mother to a thin, wiry imitation that provided food. Even a very young baby will cry for company. It won't spoil a young baby to be picked up whenever he wants. Crying also commonly occurs when his position is suddenly changed, especially if he falls back. He may also cry when his clothes are changed.

You will soon learn to recognize your baby's various cries and how to cope with them. If the crying seems high-pitched and strange, and especially if your baby is not feeding well, he may be ill and you should contact your doctor.

BOWELS

The first stool passed by your baby consists of meconium, the sticky dark green substance present in his intestine. The first meconium stool should be passed within 24 hours. Meconium derives from the amniotic fluid which the baby has swallowed while inside your womb. When feeding begins, the color and character of your baby's stools will change from dark green, almost black, to greenish brown and then to a yellowish-brown. After the fourth day he may pass four or five motions each day, and they will be yellow and semi-solid in nature. The color and consistency of the motions will vary, depending on whether you are breast or bottle feeding your baby, in which case they may look like scrambled eggs.

The number of stools passed varies greatly. Some babies fill their diapers after every meal and this is perfectly healthy. They are responding to the gastro-colic reflex which makes the bowel empty as soon as food is taken in to the stomach. Provided that your baby does not have to strain and his motions are a normal color and soft, there is no need for concern. If his motions are infrequent and hard, he simply needs a little more water to drink so give him freshly boiled water two or three times a day in quantities of, say, one tablespoon (15ml) at a time. It may be due also to too much iron in his formula, and this may need changing.

BLADDER

Most babies pass urine in the first hours after birth. The urine may contain substances called *urates* that may stain his diaper dark pink or red. Once the urine flow is established your baby may urinate as often as 20 times in 24 hours. This is because your baby's primitive bladder cannot hold urine for any length of time, not even a few minutes. This is entirely normal, and you may find the diaper wet every time you pick up your baby. Control is something which will only be learned as the bladder grows and develops. Then, and only then does your baby gain control of bladder function and start to stay dry for some length of time. Bladder control cannot be taught – i.e. potty training for very young babies is not only out of date, it is cruel.

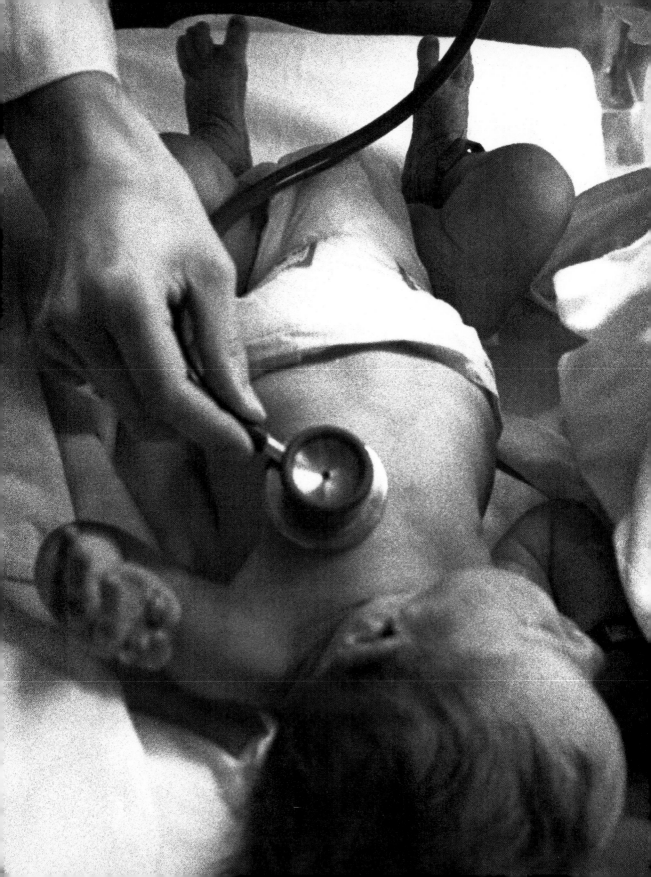

3

HOSPITAL/ HOME CARE

Like most women, you will probably have your baby in the hospital. There, you and your baby will be cared for by the medical staff. As soon as your baby is born a team of neo-natal experts will be on hand to look after her. This is to make sure that the first few seconds of life go according to plan and, after that, the first few minutes. Throughout your stay both of you will be examined regularly to make sure everything goes well.

Usually you will have your baby with you in your room, if not all the time, at least throughout the day. You may prefer, or it may be the hospital practice, to have your baby sleep in the nursery at night so that you get some rest. The amount of daily care provided by the nursing staff differs from hospital to hospital, but they should instruct you on the necessary feeding, changing and bathing routines. Other new mothers, present in the room, are also a source of support and information.

FOR THE BABY

The first job of the specialist team is to make sure that your baby breathes properly. Fetal monitoring is used to alert the medical team to any possible distress and every effort is made to prevent the baby's heartbeat from becoming depressed. These days, if babies don't begin to breathe straight away, they are put through routine resuscitation. During resuscitation your baby will get more care than at any other time in her life because the first few seconds of life are crucial, they must be monitored and your baby helped to make a flying start.

Immediately after the delivery of her head – before her body has emerged – your baby's mouth, nose and throat are cleared of mucus. The doctor or nurse sucks the mucus out using a special mucus extractor. This normal, very simple procedure is designed to ensure that her upper air passages are free from secretions when she takes her first breath.

Clearance of the nostrils is one of the most vigorous stimulants of breathing and crying. After your baby has taken her first few breaths, she may cough and bring up mucus and liquids that previously had been

ABOVE
Immediately after her head has emerged, your newborn will have her mouth, nose and throat cleared of mucus. In rare cases, she may need some oxygen to get her breathing started.

RIGHT
Once her body has emerged, the doctor will check for any congenital spinal malformations such as spina bifida.

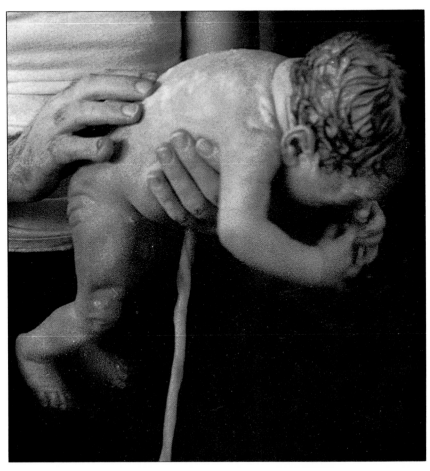

present in her lungs and trachea. This is also sucked out immediately.

Sometimes a baby has difficulties during labor or delivery and needs help at birth to breathe normally. If your baby fails to make any respiratory effort it is usually necessary to expand and ventilate her lungs. There are a number of ways this might be done. Your baby is lifted onto a resuscitation warmer, her body wrapped in blankets and her head covered so she is kept warm. Then she will be given gentle stimulation to encourage her to breathe while oxygen is directed onto her face. At this point, some babies will take their first breaths and can be brought over to you. A few need more help, and this is given by inflating your baby's lungs using a face mask which fits snuggly over her mouth and nose, and a bag that delivers volumes of oxygen. Your baby may also be resuscitated by means of a breathing tube that is passed through her mouth into her windpipe. Most babies needing resuscitation rapidly become pink and begin breathing normally quite quickly.

Although resuscitation procedures can seem to take a long time to anxious parents, they are in fact, very swift, usually taking between 5 and 15 minutes. Everything that is humanly possible will be done to make sure that your baby breathes quickly and efficiently.

IDENTI-FICATION

Before your baby leaves the delivery room, some form of identification will be fastened to her. Usually this is a plastic bracelet with either a name or number that matches yours, which is sealed around a wrist or ankle. Her footprint or palmprint may also be taken, and her crib may also be marked with her name and number. The identifying bracelet is sealed and must remain with your baby while she is in hospital. Once you are home, you may cut it to remove it.

APGAR SCORE

Your baby is vigilantly checked, and once she is born, will need to be assessed to see if any special attention is required — especially to start breathing. At one minute after birth and again five minutes later a series of five simple observations are done to provide an indication of your baby's reflexes and general well-being. The tests are measured on what is known as the Apgar scale. Developed by the late Dr. Virginia Apgar, a renowned anesthesiologist, this enables medical personnel to evaluate the condition of a newborn in double-quick time. The five areas of health the doctor will consider are:

1. Appearance (skin color). This gives the medical team an idea of how efficiently the lungs are working and if oxygenation of the blood is taking place and circulation is adequate.
2. Pulse (heart rate). This indicates the strength and regularity of the contractions of the heart.
3. Grimace/Irritability and cry (reflex). This shows how alert your baby is to stimuli.
4. Activity (movements). This gives the team a very good idea of the health and tone of your baby's muscles.
5. Respiration (breathing). This indicates the health and maturity of your baby's lungs.

The tests are scored as follows:
- Skin color (pink 2; bluish extremities 1; blue 0)
- Heart rate (above 100 beats per minute 2; below 1; absent 0)
- Reflex response (cries 2; grimace/weak movement 1; absent 0)
- Movements (active 2; some movement 1; limp 0)
- Breathing (regular 2; irregular 1; absent 0)

The higher the score the better the shape your baby is in. If your baby scores over 7, it means she is in good condition. If she scores under 4, that indicates severe distress, and she may need resuscitation. She will usually score highly when tested again a few minutes later, and almost all initially low-scoring babies turn out normal and healthy.

PHYSICAL EXAMIN-ATIONS AND TESTS

Shortly after birth, in addition to the Apgar tests, your baby will be examined by the doctor so that her general condition is assessed. The doctor will check to make sure her facial features and body proportions are normal. She will be turned over so the doctor can see that the back is normal and there is no spina bifida. Her anus and legs will be examined and her fingers and toes checked. The number of blood vessels in the umbilical

Within a day or so of birth your baby will be given a more thorough examination than the one performed right after delivery. The doctor will usually start at the head and work down to the feet.

Her or she will listen to the baby's heart and lungs to check that they are functioning properly. Many babies have a heart murmur immediately after birth which usually clears up within a few days.

The doctor will also examine the arms and legs, and check that the baby does not have a congenital hip dislocation. He or she will also examine the baby's mouth (to check for conditions such as cleft palate).

If the doctor finds something abnormal, additional tests such as an ultrasound scan may be necessary. This is not an indication that there is something seriously wrong with your baby but simply that the doctor wants to investigate further.

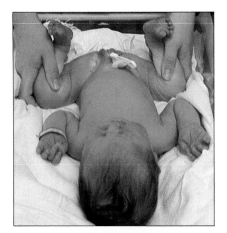
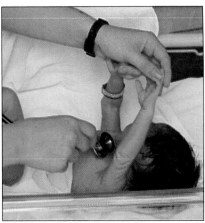
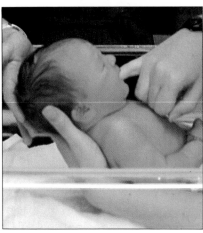
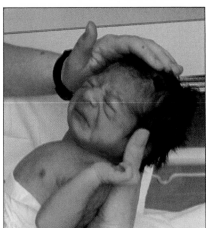

cord is recorded; normally there are two arteries and one vein. Next comes the weighing of your baby; her head and body length will be measured. Her temperature will be checked with a rectal thermometer and she will be warmed, if she needs it. This preliminary examination takes only a few seconds in the hands of an experienced doctor. You then can be assured that your baby is healthy and normal.

Your baby is more thoroughly examined about 24 hours after birth. This is because your baby could easily become cold during a prolonged examination in the delivery room, and because there can be misleading signs in the hour or so after birth.

The more thorough examination takes place when the baby is warm and settled. Make sure that you are with your baby at this time by getting staff to alert you when it's going to take place, as it gives you an opportunity to ask the doctor any questions, and to tell your doctor any worries you might have. The baby is placed on a flat surface in a good light and at a convenient height for the comfort of the doctor, who may be seated. If you cannot be present always ask for the results of the examination. There are different ways of checking a newborn baby but generally the doctor will start at the top of the head and work down to the toes.

Head and neck
The doctor will examine:
1. The head for the presence of any molding or misshaping during delivery through the birth canal.
2. The skull bones and the fontanelles.
3. Your baby's eyes, ears, nose and mouth.
4. The gums and palate for any evidence of congenital abnormality such as cleft palate.
5. Your baby's mouth for any teeth (although most newborns do not have teeth, if any are present that are loose or coming through at an unusual angle, they are usually removed in case they fall out and are inhaled by the baby).
6. Your baby's neck for any cysts or swellings.

Chest and heart
The doctor will listen to the heart and lungs with a stethoscope to make sure that the lungs are properly expanded and working normally. Most of the noises heard immediately after delivery will have disappeared. Many babies have a heart murmur for the first two or three days of life. If your doctor mentions this, do not worry, as the vast majority disappear quite spontaneously and very quickly. If there is a murmur, it will be noted and checked when you bring your baby in for the post-natal check-up, unless it is considered potentially serious in which case she will be investigated more extensively in the hospital.

Breasts
Engorgement or swelling of the breasts is very common in full-term babies of both sexes. Many babies have breast enlargement of various degrees that lasts two to three days after birth. It is not serious, and requires no treatment. The enlargement is due to the baby's own hormone activity after the withdrawal of the comparatively huge amounts of maternal

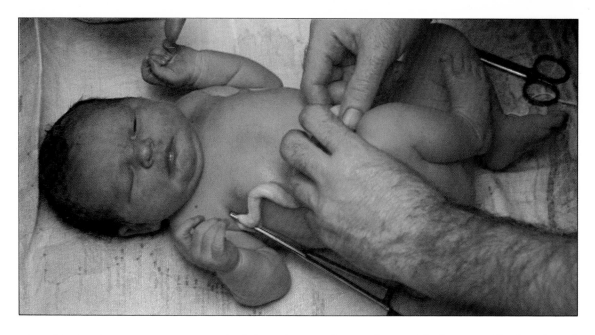

The umbilical cord will be moist and bluish-white at birth. It will be clamped and then cut with scissors. Only a short length of cord will remain, which will dry and become almost black within two to four hours. The stump will dry, shrivel up and fall off about seven days after birth. This process is painless to your baby.

estrogens which have been in the circulation. The breasts of both girls and boys may even discharge a small amount of a milky substance.

Arms and hands

The pulse in each arm is felt and a check made for normal movement and strength. You will notice that the doctor will check your baby's fingers and palm creases. Nearly all babies have two major creases across each palm. A single crease alerts the doctor to look for other physical abnormalities and these will be investigated.

Abdomen and genitals

The doctor will

1. Palpate (feel deeply with the whole length of the fingers) gently the abdominal wall to check the condition of the liver and spleen, both of which may be slightly enlarged in the newborn baby, and to ensure there are no ruptures.
2. If your baby is a boy, check the testes to ensure that they are properly descended.
3. If your baby is a girl, check her genitalia to ensure that the labia are not joined together and the clitoris is a normal size. A baby girl may have some white vaginal discharge, which may become slightly bloodstained after a few days as the baby's hormone levels drop.
4. Feel the pulse in your baby's groin.
5. Turn the baby over to check the lower spine and anus to see if there is a congenital defect, an opening that might need repair, or whether the anus is not opened. There may be a small harmless dimple or pit over the spine just behind the anus which needs no treatment.
6. Check that your baby has had a bowel movement and passed urine during the first 24 hours.

BABY RACHEL

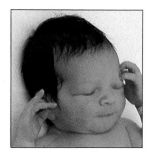

Born: four days after expected date of delivery

Weight: 7lb 4oz (3250g)

Condition: was a "slow starter;" needed to have some oxygen

Mother's labor: lasted 15 hours; was longer than mother expected

Feeding: bottle fed

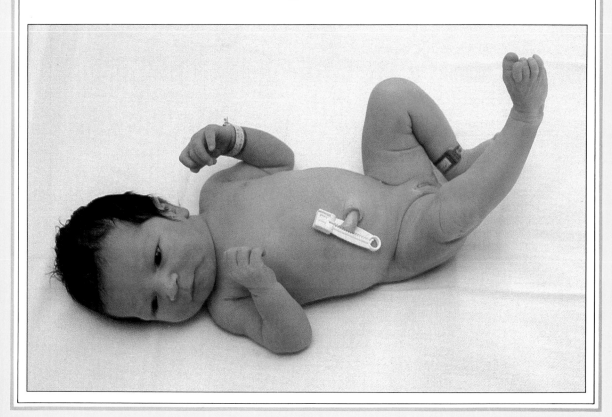

THE FIRST DAY

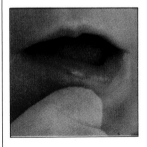

"She was lovely and feminine-looking right from the start. She had very smooth skin. But in all other ways she was just like her brothers".

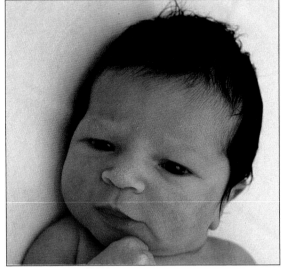

"She is our fourth baby. I already had 3 boys. I wanted 4 children and didn't mind if it was another boy and, in fact, I was surprised she was a girl. I sort of thought I could only have boys!".

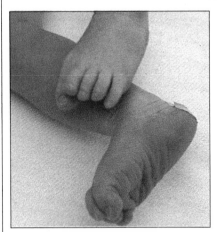

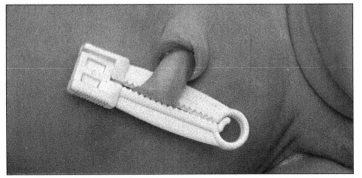

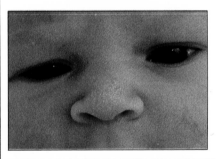

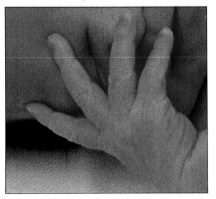

"I think my husband wanted a girl. The first couple of weeks he treated her as if she was china — he was slightly overprotective. Now he treats her like all the others".

THE TENTH DAY

"She had sharp needle-like nails and was covered in scratches while she was in hospital. Although we didn't notice it at the time because of the clamp on her cord, she has an umbilical hernia. The doctor says it will probably get better by itself and won't need surgery".

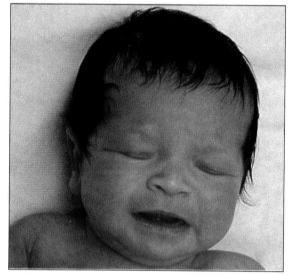

"She had masses of hair when she was born and she still does. Everyone said it would fall out but I told them it wouldn't and it didn't".

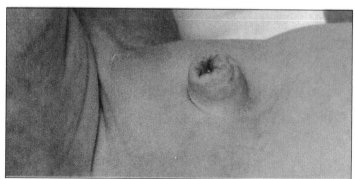

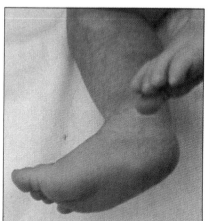

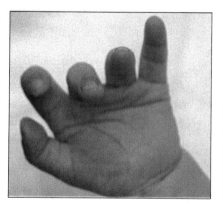

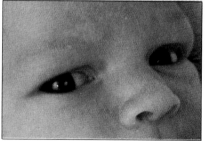

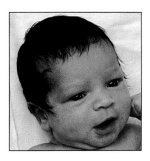

"She's a good sleeper, good feeder and very contented. She's gained weight very rapidly. She's also a very noisy, gurgling baby and very wide awake. She likes all the activity provided by her three brothers. After she was born she stayed awake for three to four hours — just looking not crying. I was amazed".

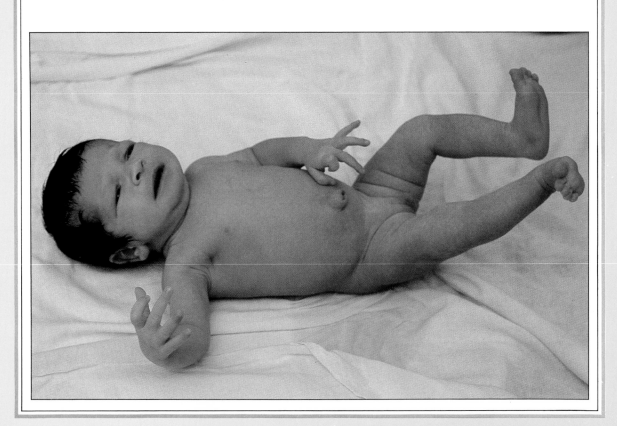

The hips, legs and feet

1. Your baby will be tested to see if congenital dislocation of the hip is present. Your doctor will hold her thighs firmly and move each leg to see whether the head of the thigh bone is unstable or lies outside the hip joint. If so, she will need to be seen by specialists. Congenital dislocation of the hip can usually be treated successfully in the weeks after birth. Testing the hips is not painful for the baby though she may cry because of the disturbance of having her legs moved about.

2. Your baby's legs and feet will be examined to see that they are of equal length and size. If the ankle is still held in the position it had in the uterus your baby may have club foot (a misshapen or twisted foot treated by manipulation and the application of a cast). Newborn babies are curled up very tightly after having been in the uterus for so long and it may take them some while to stretch out. It was only on the sixth day that I saw my first son completely straightened out. He'd been curled up so tightly that I'd imagined he was about 15 inches long whereas he turned out to be nearly 20 inches.

Nerves and muscles

1. Your baby's nerves and muscles will be assessed by putting her arms and legs through a range of movements to make sure that they are not too stiff or too floppy.

2. Her head control will be checked and her reflexes may also be assessed. These reflexes include sucking, grasping, stepping, placing and the Moro reflex (see Reflexes p.37).

GOING HOME FROM THE HOSPITAL

Hospital practice varies, but whether you leave the hospital after 48 hours or six days, your baby will have been thoroughly examined by a pediatrician to make sure that everything is going well. Your doctor will want to check that she is feeding well (or attempting to feed if you are only in the hospital overnight) and that her eliminations are normal. She may be given a blood test for phenylketonuria (PKU), a rare metabolic disease that causes mental retardation, and also for thyroid gland underactivity (hypothyroidism).

FOR THE MOTHER

AFTER THE DELIVERY

Your care routine will vary, depending on whether you had a vaginal or cesarean delivery (see below), whether you were at home or in the hospital, which hospital you were in, and your condition.

Immediately after delivery your temperature will be taken and your pulse rate and blood pressure recorded. They will continue to be recorded every 4 hours for the first day or so, then about twice daily for the next week, in the hospital or at home. Your temperature and pulse may rise on the third or fourth day after delivery if your breasts become engorged.

Medical staff will also check that any stitches or tears are healing properly and that there is no infection. They may also advise you on applying ice packs to the area to prevent swelling and prescribe pain killers during the first few days for after-pains.

The amount and appearance of lochia, the post-childbirth bloody discharge (see p.79), will be regularly monitored by staff checking the sanitary pads you will be given. They will want to make sure that there are no abnormal blood clots or excessive bleeding. They will also check the condition of your uterus to ensure that it is starting to return to its pre-pregnant condition. Your doctor will also examine you for signs of thrombosis (by squeezing your calves), and will also check your general emotional state.

The nursing staff will want to know that you are urinating regularly and that you've had at least one bowel movement before leaving the hospital. Occasionally, especially after a long or difficult labor, particularly if forceps were used, you may have difficulty urinating because of bruising around the bladder. Usually, in the hospital, the first method used to get you to start passing urine is simply to let water run, and this works for about 80 per cent of women. The nursing staff may pass a catheter and remove it soon after, or leave it for several hours or days, as necessary.

Many women become slightly constipated during the time after delivery because a lot of fluid is lost from the body and the rectum reabsorbs as much water as possible from the feces to keep the body fluids balanced. Therefore, the nursing staff will probably give you a cellulose-based medicine that will bind water into the stool to soften it. If you have had an episiotomy, the stitches may cause a natural reluctance to exert any

During your stay in the hospital you will be examined on a regular basis. Your blood pressure and temperature will be checked daily, and blood tests may be performed to make certain you have not developed an infection following delivery. These visits with the nurse or doctor are a good opportunity to ask any questions or discuss any worries you might have.

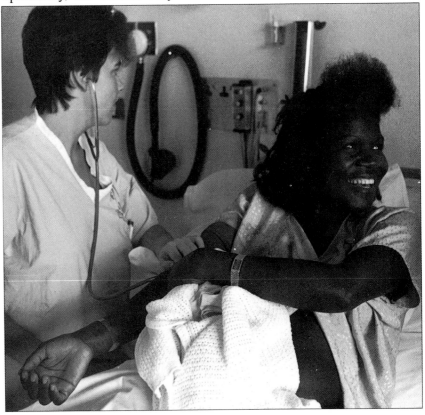

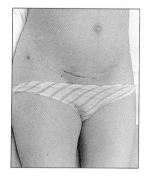

ABOVE
If you have a cesarean delivery, the scar is usually horizontal or transverse just above the pubic bone about 6 or 7 in across. This is often called a "bikini" incision. In rare cases, for special medical reasons you may have a vertical incision (from just below the navel to the pubic bone). Your incision will have been sutured with absorbable material, layer by layer.

RIGHT
Side effects of a cesarean performed under general anesthesia include drowsiness, a sore throat (from a tube which is usually placed down your mouth and throat to assist breathing), and a dry mouth. If you have had a regional anesthetic, such as an epidural, you may have a loss of feeling in your legs. In both cases, you will feel pain at the incision site once the anesthesia wears off. You will also have vaginal bleeding because lochia will flow from your uterus.

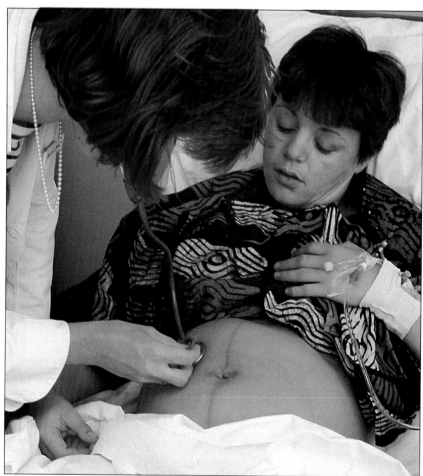

pressure. You may need to be prescribed additional medication to keep the bowels regular as well as eating sufficient roughage.

More and more doctors are encouraging new mothers to move about as much as possible soon after delivery. Early mobility will help you regain your strength more quickly and facilitates bowel and bladder function. You will probably remain in bed for the first six hours and then be allowed up to go the toilet, shower or walk about. When you first get up you may experience a frightening sudden gush of blood. This is blood that has pooled in your vagina while you were lying down. Therefore, it is wise to ask for assistance the first time you get out of bed, as you could feel faint or weak from this sudden loss of blood.

Blood tests are often routinely taken on about the second day after delivery to ensure that your hemoglobin is returning to normal.

CESAREAN MOTHERS

About 20–25 per cent of women have cesarean births in the U.S. You may have little reaction from an epidural anesthetic but if you had general, you may feel tired and confused; in all cases the incision will be sore. The stitches will probably be low down across the bikini line but the doctor may have made a vertical incision. In either case, the stitches will be covered by a soft dressing. (Another technique involves the use of surgical clamps or clips to close the incision. The edges of the scar fuse together before the clamps or clips are removed painlessly.) You will probably have an intravenous drip in your arm, and you will be given some pain relief medication to allow you to get some sleep. The medication will be a kind that doesn't enter your colostrum and you'll be free of medicines by the time your milk comes in.

To improve your circulation prop yourself up with pillows, sit up straight and take frequent deep breaths. It is essential for your circulation to move your feet and legs after any operation. You can do this in bed by vigorously bending and stretching your ankles a few times, circling your feet around and around, and bending alternate legs. Ask your doctor about when to practice post-natal exercises. If your stitches are not self-absorbing, they will be removed about five or six days after delivery with only mild discomfort. After a cesarean, you will usually stay in the hospital for about four to six days.

GOING HOME FROM THE HOSPITAL

The routine for going home will vary from hospital to hospital. Some women leave quite soon after the birth, others are in for over a week. The normal stay is three days for a normal vaginal birth, and six days for a cesarean birth. You may be able to go into hospital for 48 hours only; decide before your labor what your preference is.

Before you are discharged:

● A doctor will examine you to see that your uterus is returning to its pre-pregnant size, that your stitches, if any, are healing, and that your breasts are normal. He or she will want to know that your eliminations are normal. You will probably be asked about the amount and color of your vaginal discharge (*lochia*), and it will be examined to see if you have passed any clots. Clotting accompanied by persistant, heavy bleeding may indicate that some placental tissue has been retained in the abdomen.

● If you have had a cesarean, your incision will be checked and any non-absorbable sutures will be removed.

● You will be asked about contraception at a postpartum office visit, four to six weeks after delivery, and you will be given a prescription if needed. You should have decided what form of contraception you want to use after you've had your baby *before* you go into labor.

● If you weren't immune to rubella (german measles) during your pregnancy you may be immunised. The vaccination will not affect your milk.

● A nurse or midwife will show you how to clean your baby's umbilical cord if it has not already dropped off.

● You will be given a date for your post-natal check-up, and advised to take your baby to the pediatrician for a two-, four- or six-week developmental check-up.

Your doctor will also examine you to make sure that your uterus is returning to its pre-pregnant state. He or she may do this by palpating your abdomen to feel the size and position of your uterus.

Pelvic exercises like the ones you did while you were pregnant will help your muscles return to normal. These can usually be started a few days after delivery (unless you had a cesarean). If you did not learn these exercises during pre-natal classes, your doctor will be able to show you how to do them.

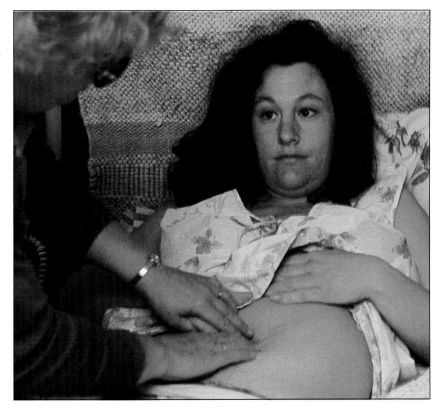

BIRTH CERTIFICATES

By U.S. law, a birth certificate must be filled out in the hospital after every birth. The certificate includes all the medical details of the birth, and is signed by the obstetrician. In addition, the baby's parents are given a form to fill in while they are in the hospital. This form, giving the full names and data of the parents, and the name and sex of the newborn baby, is retained by the hospital. Within about four to six weeks of leaving the hospital, the parents are sent an official birth certificate by mail.

4
CHANGES IN YOU

Once your baby is here, and the initial euphoria and excitement wears off slightly, you may be aware suddenly of how you actually feel.

A number of physical and emotional changes happen to you after childbirth. Some are due to radical hormonal changes when all your pregnancy hormones, including those secreted by the placenta, are suddenly withdrawn; others are a result of the birth process itself, and then there is the emotional impact of having a new baby and another member of the family. While the majority of physical changes are rapid and dramatic, it will be at least nine months before your body completely returns to its normal non-pregnant state. This is particularly applicable if you are breastfeeding.

The puerperium is defined as the period after childbirth during which the body returns to its normal non-pregnant state. This is usually four to six weeks. It is mainly during the first few days after delivery that the most dramatic changes occur. After a week the return to normality continues to be steady and automatic.

You will probably be very emotional immediately after the birth. Most mothers are tired but ecstatic with their new babies. You may feel incredible joy and relief that your baby is healthy and normal. You and your partner will certainly be thrilled about the new, long-awaited addition to your family. But not all women react so positively. It is quite normal that some women may have a distinct lack of interest in their babies. Such depressed feelings are usually due to the effects of anesthesia, and exhaustion if labor was hard and prolonged. However, mother love will assert itself; just give it a chance.

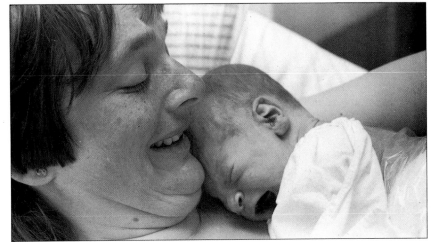

RIGHT
If your baby was premature or needs special care, it may be more difficult to establish bonding as you will not be able to have your baby with you all the time. You will need to make the effort to visit your baby in the special care ward. Ask if you can hold and feed him to increase the amount of physical contact you have.

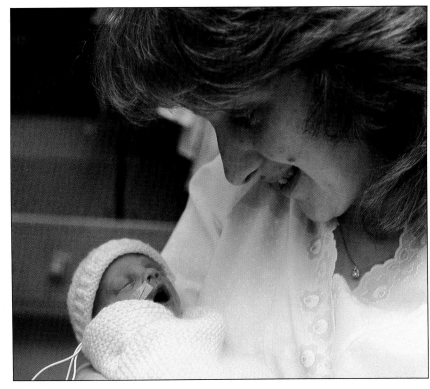

BELOW
After birth you will certainly be exhausted and tired, but happy to have your new baby with you. Your baby will also be tired, so don't worry if he does not seem to respond to you in the way you would like him to.

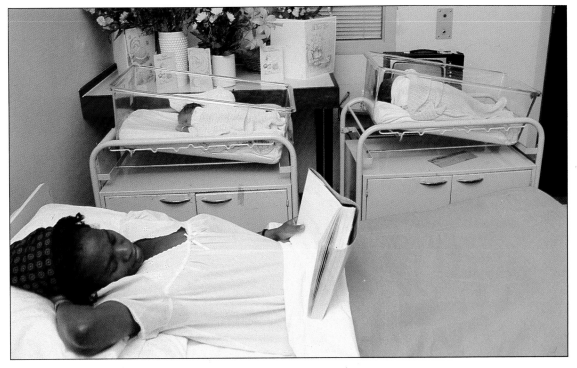

Birth is a wonderful experience but you may find it overwhelming. You may discover that you are exhausted and only want to sleep instead of celebrate. This is a very common phenomenon, and is often known as the "baby blues". The changes in your hormone levels may leave you feeling tired and depressed. Almost all women suffer these emotions to some degree, mostly due to the change in routine, the pressure and excitement of a new baby, and the lack of sleep.

Make sure that you get some time to yourself if you need it. Ask that visitors be restricted if you need some time alone.

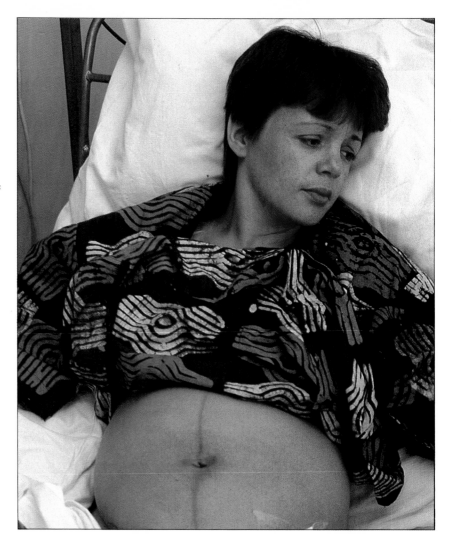

STITCHES

If you had an episiotomy, which is when the doctor cuts the perineum to prevent tearing during birth, or if you have sustained a tear, you will undoubtedly have stitches. Quite soon after birth, any anesthetic will wear off and your stitches will begin to hurt. This is because they shrink as they heal and pull the surrounding skin. The site of the wound will take time to heal, usually about seven to ten days, and during that time you will be checked to make sure there is no inflammation.

Many hospitals have blow-up donut cushions for you to put down wherever you sit for the first days after birth. A cushion helps to ease the tension in the sore skin around the stitches.

It is important, in order to prevent infection, to practice correct postpartum perineal hygiene. Make sure that you do the following:
● Use a fresh sanitary pad at least every four to six hours, secured snugly, so that it doesn't slide back and forth. Remove it from front to back to

avoid dragging germs from the anal area to the vagina.
● Pour or squirt warm water, or an antiseptic solution if suggested by your doctor, over the area after urinating or defecating. Pat dry with gauze pads or with paper wipes. Always wipe from front to back.
● Your doctor may prescribe sitz baths. You can take warm salt baths or apply hot compresses.
● Apply chilled witch hazel on a sterile gauze pad, or use prepared witch hazel pads, available from most drug stores.
● Use local anesthetics in spray, cream or pad form, or mild pain relievers, if your doctor allows.
● Lie on your side. Avoid standing for long periods of time and sitting in the same position. This will decrease any strain on the area. Sitting on a pillow or an inflated donut ring may help, as may tightening your buttocks before sitting.
● Do your pelvic exercises (see below) as frequently as possible in order to stimulate circulation in the area, promote healing and improve muscle tone. You may not be able to feel the pressure of the muscles immediately as the area will be numb immediately after delivery. Feeling will return to the perineum gradually over the next few weeks.

LOCHIA

Lochia is the vaginal discharge expelled from the uterus after delivery. Immediately following delivery the lochia is bright red. The quantity of bleeding for the first few hours after delivery will be about the same amount as a normal period, or even slightly more. Occasionally a few small blood clots are passed. The lochia remains red for the first few two or three days and then gradually changes to reddish brown, and by the fourth or fifth day the lochia will be brown. When you get up and start to be more active, the color may change and for a short while be red again. This is quite normal, and the color will change back to pink or brown within a few hours, or days.

There is no standard duration for lochia to continue following delivery. In some women it stops after about 14 days whereas in others it may continue for as long as six weeks. The average is about 21 days. Frequently, especially if the baby is not breastfed, the lochia finishes after the first period which comes approximately four weeks after delivery.

The amount and color of the lochia indicate how quickly the uterus is returning to its normal condition and size. The more rapidly the uterus changes, the more rapidly the lochia will turn brown and cease altogether. Breastfeeding helps the uterus to return to normal more rapidly and the lochia will dry up more quickly in a woman who is breastfeeding.

Tampons cannot be worn until about six weeks after birth so you will need to wear sanitary napkins or pads. These will be supplied by the hospital, though you will need to check before birth. Special post-maternity pads are sold commercially, or you can use super size.

BREASTS

There will be no dramatic or sudden change in your breasts immediately after delivery or for the first 24 hours. Colostrum, the yellow fluid secreted by the breasts before the actual milk flows in, is an ideal food for newborn babies though to you it may appear thin, clear and insubstantial. Early encouragement will help your baby to suckle at your breasts for a short time, to get it going. During the second day after delivery your breasts may begin to fill and become firmer and heavier. On the third day the breasts usually start to produce milk in reasonable amounts. They may become quite firm and even tender and will certainly increase considerably in size. You should wear a good supportive bra.

If you are not going to breastfeed, you might be given a pill or injection containing antilactogenic hormone to dry up your milk or, you may be told to wear a very tight bra and place ice packs on your breasts. It is a good idea to avoid drinking too many liquids as this encourages milk production.

WEIGHT

You will automatically lose a certain amount of weight after delivery. The average is about 15 lb, consisting of the baby, the placenta, amniotic fluid, and some of the extra blood that was circulating in your body. More weight is lost as your uterus gradually returns to normal in the two weeks after delivery. Don't expect to fit into your regular clothes within the first few days after childbirth. Your abdomen will be distended and flabby for a number of days, if not weeks.

INABILITY TO SLEEP

You may find that you do not sleep well for the first few days after delivery. The excitement and strain of labor and delivery, thinking about your new baby, and the changes happening in your body may all combine to throw your system off. Report any insomnia to your doctor.

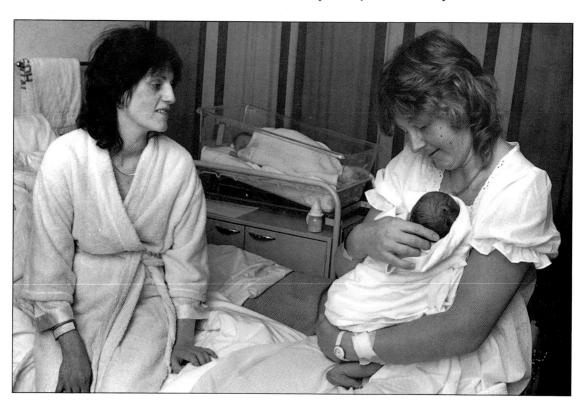

ELIMIN-ATIONS

Anesthetics given during childbirth or immediately after delivery can affect your ability to empty your bladder successfully, as can stitches. Often, one cannot tell whether the bladder is full or if it has emptied completely. To stimulate urination and avoid being catheterized, contract and release your pelvic floor muscles five times every 15 or 20 minutes.

You may not have a bowel movement until a few days after the birth especially if you had not eaten much when labor began. Be aware, however, that you may avoid moving your bowels if you have had an episiotomy and worry that it will be uncomfortable. To prevent straining, drink plenty of liquid and eat fresh fruit and whole grain cereals. If hemorrhoids are present, apply an anesthetic ointment or specially-treated gauze pads, and have warm baths if your doctor agrees.

SKIN AND HAIR

You may notice brownish or reddish stretch marks on your abdomen, breasts, buttocks or thighs. These *striae* gradually shrink and become paler within four to six months but you will be left with some pearly-white marks. On the other hand, any increased pigmentation that appeared during pregnancy will fade away as will any distended capillaries that might have appeared underneath your skin.

Some months after childbirth you may experience what appears to be excessive hair loss from the scalp. This is due to your hormone levels returning to their pre-pregnant state and such loss is only temporary.

EMOTIONS

After the high levels of hormones circulating in your blood during pregnancy, the enormous swing to lower levels often causes women to become tearful, moody, anxious, irritable, and depressed. About half of new mothers suffer this type of depression and there is no reason to worry about it. The postpartum "baby blues" usually last for no longer than a week. If your unhappiness lasts any longer, contact your doctor immediately because the longer the depression goes on, the more difficult it is to treat satisfactorily.

If your depression is severe (which is very rare), persists for more than two weeks, and is accompanied by difficulty in sleeping and lack of appetite, or begins some weeks after the baby is born, consult your doctor. Don't allow the feelings to drag on, thinking they will disappear.

You may find it difficult to cope with your new baby, and be overwhelmed by the responsibility. You will probably be very tired, and worried about not being able to get everything done. These contribute to your feelings of depression. You may also have a decresed blood count due to blood loss at delivery, and this contributes to your feelings of exhaustion. Your muscles will not work as efficiently as usual and they will feel weak and tire easily. Remember, it will take several weeks to return to normal. To help avoid exhaustion:

● Always get enough rest. Lie down with your feet up. Make it an absolute rule and negotiate with your partner and relatives to get enough sleep, including asking a friend to live in for the first couple of weeks. Best of all, ask your mother if you get on with her or your mother-in-law, or a woman relative whom you're close to. Don't ignore signs of tiredness. Stop what you are doing if it is not essential and lie down with your feet up.

● You don't have to sleep to regain your strength. Just lying and resting

In most maternity wards you will be sharing a room with other new mothers. This gives you an opportunity to ask questions and discuss your feelings with other women who are going through the same experience as you.

The arrival of twins can be overwhelming even if you are prepared. The fact that there are two babies who need feeding, changing and attention can be very difficult at first. You will need to work out some schedules to make sure that both babies are cared for and to ensure that you have enough time to yourself. You may need to arrange for special help at home for the first few days until you establish your routine. Your doctor will be able to give you tips on how to cope, and can put you in touch with organizations who can offer specific help and advice.

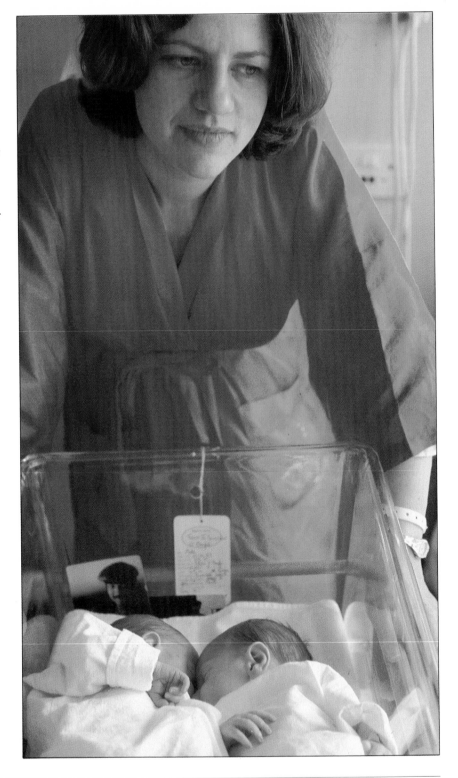

At the beginning, motherhood appears to be an all-consuming role; it is important for you to spend all the available time on yourself and your baby. Once home, you will be able to manage many more things, but for a long time to come, life will never be the same again!

will give your heart and lungs and other vital organs a chance to recover.

● Whether in home or the hospital, have somebody to help you with the chores, housework and new baby during the early days so you can rest.

● Discourage visitors if you are unable to cope. Put yourself and your baby first, and ask to be left alone.

It is a good idea, therefore, to ward off any impending depression by putting yourself together as quickly as possible after the birth. Take a shower as soon as you can; wash your hair if it makes you feel better. Put on one of your own pretty nightgowns (if breastfeeding, have one that buttons down the front) and put on make-up if you normally wear it. Should you experience mood swings that bother you, just remind yourself these will soon pass and you'll be back being yourself.

5
FEEDING YOUR BABY

Your baby, particularly if she has a low birth weight, say under seven pounds, may need more frequent feeding than you imagined, and for the first days of life, you must follow your baby's demands. You will get nowhere in the first 72 hours by trying to give exactly timed four-hourly feeds, regardless of what the nursing staff tells you, so follow your baby's needs and you may find that she feeds about every two to two-and-a-half hours, having as many as eight to ten feeds a day. But, by about one month, your baby may be taking food every four hours and going even longer by the end of three months. However, each baby is different with its own needs and appetites.

Make sure you decide on breastfeeding or bottle feeding before you go into labor and tell the staff what you intend to do. They will be able to help you and answer any questions you might have about problems or technique. (Also, they may wish to give you medication to dry up your milk should you decide to bottle feed).

In many hospitals, visitors are not permitted during feeding times, primarily to protect babies from possible infection. Enjoy this private time together getting to know each other better.

Mother's milk is the ideal food for newborns, as it contains the right amount of nutrients to sustain your baby. It also contains antibodies to protect your baby from certain infections and diseases. It is easily digested and breastfed babies don't usually get constipated.

You will be able to put your baby to your breast immediately after birth. This physical closeness helps you to bond with your baby and the baby's sucking helps to stimulate the production of milk (which usually comes in about three days after delivery). This closeness helps your baby to identify you by touch, sound and smell.

Until the milk comes in, your baby will be taking in only colostrum, which contains antibodies to help protect your baby against illnesses and infections.

A newborn baby has a broad flat nose and receding chin and jaw to facilitate breast feeding. This allows your baby to breathe comfortably through her nose while she is feeding through her mouth.

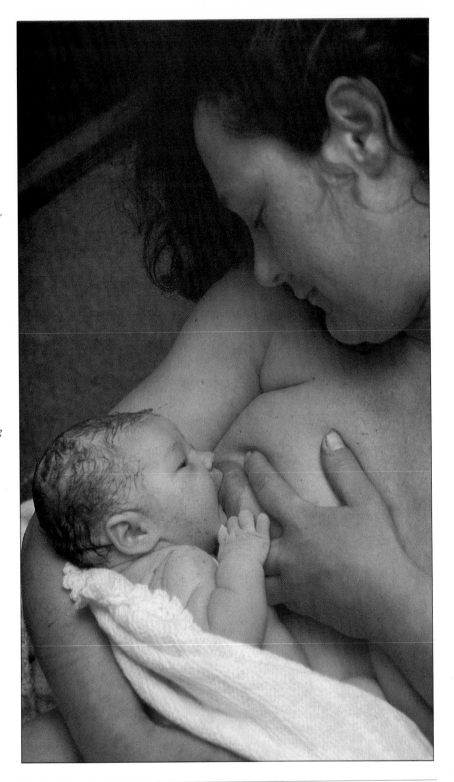

BREAST-FEEDING

There are a number of good reasons to breastfeed. Breast milk is the ideal food for your newborn baby. It has the correct amount of nutrients to provide your baby with all that she needs. In addition, breast milk contains various antibodies that help to protect your baby from disease later in life, including chest infections, gastroenteritis and colds, in fact, all the infections you've been exposed to. Breast milk is easily digested, and less likely to cause stomach upsets and diarrhea. No matter what size or shape your breasts, you will be able to produce enough milk to feed your baby, or both, if you have twins, and breastfeeding helps you develop strong bonds with your baby in the first few days. You can easily express breast milk so that the father can be involved in the feeding process. Breastfeeding helps your uterus return to its pre-pregnant size more quickly, and also uses up the extra fat that your body stored during pregnancy, especially on the thighs and the upper arms. The latest research has shown that those jodhpur thighs you're so eager to get rid of are actually a fat store to provide milk for your baby, so if you want to get rid of them, breastfeed; you'll never get rid of them by bottle feeding.

The routine varies from hospital to hospital but the baby is usually put to the breast four times on the first day and five or six times on the second day. Everyone should start slowly at first with only short periods, possibly just two or three minutes, on each breast so that the breasts have a chance to harden up. This stops soreness and cracking. When your baby is put to the breast on the third day, usually every four hours, she will suck off the milk and your breasts will become less tender and sore.

Help your baby the first few times to find your nipple. Cradle your baby in your arms and gently stroke the cheek nearest your breast. This will

Each baby feeds differently. It takes most a few days to get used to the process, and you may have some problems getting feeding established. Your baby may appear uninterested in feeding and sleep through feeds. She may even refuse the breast. Other babies are aggressive when they feed, sucking vigorously, or want to feed all the time. If your baby appears anxious or startled when you pick her up to feed her, hold her firmly and talk soothingly all the time. Pick her up gently and slowly to allow her to get used to being picked up.

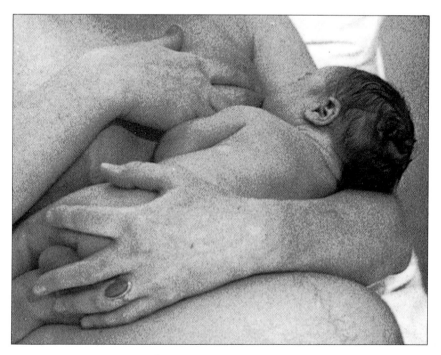

RIGHT
Wear comfortable clothes when you are nursing. Shirts that button down the front or that can be lifted up easily are ideal because it makes your breasts accessible. You should also wear a good fitting bra since your breasts will become very large and heavy when filled with milk.

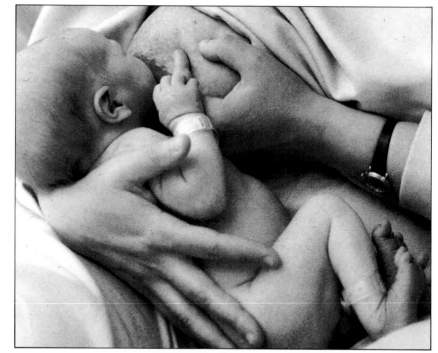

BELOW
When nursing twins you may need some help establishing a pattern. Some mothers prefer to feed twins one at a time, changing breasts halfway through a feeding. Others prefer to feed both babies at once, one on each breast.

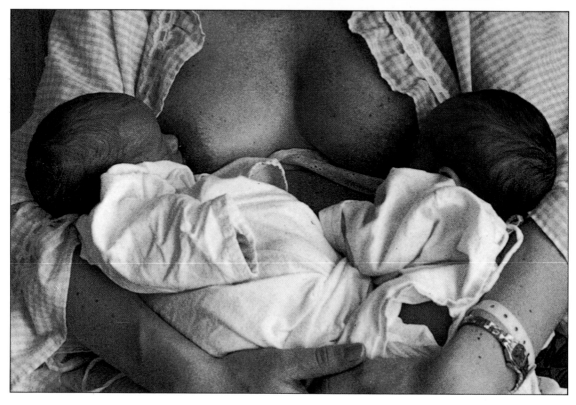

You can feed your baby in any position you choose as long as your baby can fix on the nipple and you are comfortable and relaxed. You can sit with your back propped up against the back of a chair or sofa, or you may prefer to lie down with your baby alongside of you, especially if you've had a cesarean. Cradle your baby in your arm, with her head in the crook of your elbow and her back and botton supported by your hand.

When feeding, try and make the experience as comfortable as you can for your baby. If possible, the room should be quiet with no bright lights. Try to keep the distractions to a minimum, especially in the early days when you are establishing a routine. Talk, sing or croon to your baby, who will be soothed by the sound of your voice.

elicit the rooting reflex and your baby will turn her head towards your breast, and open her mouth. After a few days, your baby will need no incentive or stimulation. She will latch onto your breast as soon as she is held close to the body.

Be sure when you first begin to get the nipple well inside your baby's mouth. Unless a large proportion of the areola is inside, the milk will not be successfully sucked out. Also, if your nipple is positioned well inside the baby's mouth you minimize the chance of developing sore nipples.

Your baby's sucking is strongest in the first five minutes of feeding; your baby takes in 80 per cent of her feed then. Keep your baby on the breast for as long as she shows interest in sucking, but not usually longer than 10 minutes on each breast. Your breast will probably have emptied by then and she may just enjoy the sensation of sucking. You may find that your baby loses interest in her own way. She may start to play with the breast, taking her mouth on and off the nipple, she may turn away or even fall asleep. When she has had enough of one, gently take the baby off your nipple and put her to the other breast. If your baby falls asleep after feeding from both breasts she has probably had enough.

To remove the baby from your breast, never pull her off. This will only hurt your nipple. Gently loosen her mouth by pressing gently but firmly on her chin. Alternatively, slip your finger down between the areola and your baby's cheek and put your little finger into the corner of your baby's mouth. Both techniques will make the mouth open and the breast will slip out easily. This is important in the first few days of feeding as the nipple is

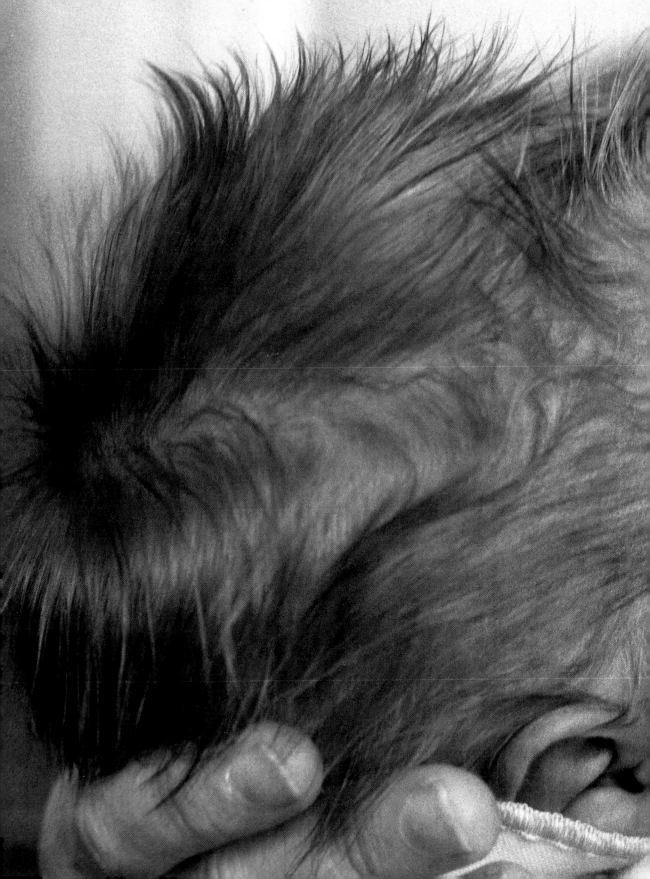

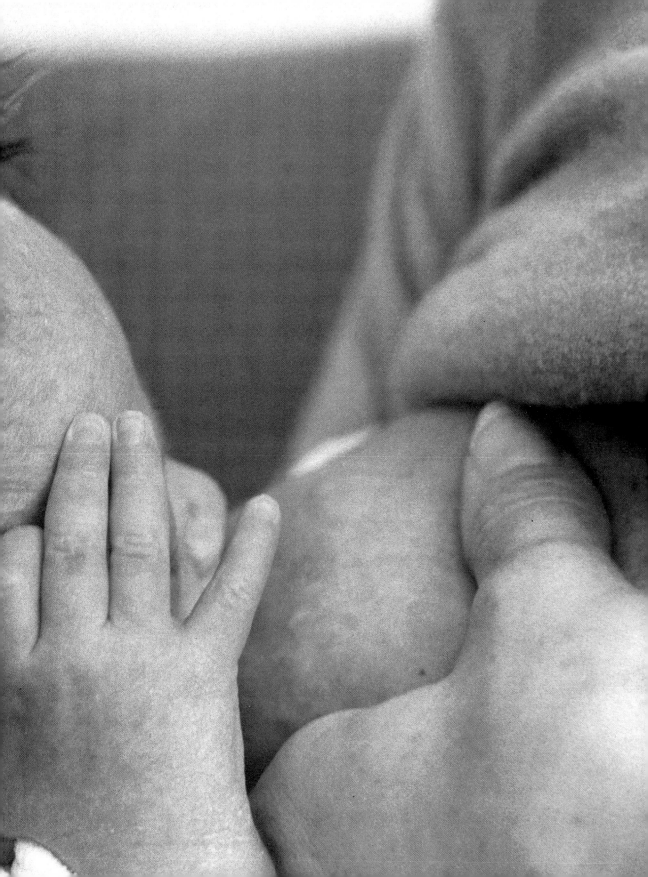

rather soft and needs a chance to harden.

If you had a cesarean birth it may not be comfortable to cuddle and hold your baby. Instead, try tucking your baby under your arm so that her legs and body are by your side and her face towards your breast. If necessary, use a pillow to raise her up.

PROBLEMS WITH FEEDING

You may find that your baby is fine between feedings but then becomes playful, difficult, unsettled as soon as you put her on the breast and she's had a few sucks. This is usually because the baby is picking up your feelings so don't think about her as being difficult; think about what is going on inside yourself. Are you tired, worried, frustrated, anxious? Try to make sure that you spend a few minutes calming yourself down, looking forward to the feed, anticipating the joy of it before you actually start. Your baby will always pick up your mood whatever it is, and it is better that she picks up a good one.

Some doctors feel that irritability is due to the baby finding it difficult to breathe because her nose may be obstructed by being buried in the breast or because her upper lip is pressed back against her nostrils. Therefore, you must first, with the help of a nurse, ensure your baby is in the proper feeding position. Feed your baby as soon as she appears hungry, rather than letting the irritation grow, and pick her up and cuddle her as often as you can before a feeding. Handle her with the utmost firmness, and gently place her on the breast. Encourage your baby to want the food and to perform the rooting reflex by stroking her cheek gently before you put her on to the breast, then she will be eager and take the food more smoothly. Don't hurry your baby. Remain calm and eventually your baby will settle down and feed successfully.

On the other hand, your baby may be a drowsy one that falls asleep after feeding from just one side. You may find it impossible to awaken her gently. It will be annoying for you if she wakes up shortly after feeling hungry and crying. The best thing to do is to shorten the feeding time so that she is made to suck for less than 10 minutes on the first breast.

Gas in babies is due to their inability to regulate their intake of air with the milk and is often the result of an unduly rapid flow of milk from the breast. This can be helped by expressing a small quantity when your breast is distended. Feeding your newborn in an upright position will enable air to rise more rapidly.

Your baby may also refuse the breast if there has been a delay in starting to feed after birth. The sooner you start the better. Babies learn to take the breast quickly in the first 48 hours after birth but find it more difficult the longer feeding is left. My suggestion is that you give your baby the first feeding within the first four hours of birth so that you both get used to it quickly. In addition, your baby may simply be worried or distracted.

Start feeding gently and don't startle your baby. In fact, start by talking soothingly for a few minutes. This will calm you both down. When feeding, keep the room quiet and comfortable. Avoid feeding when there are disturbing noises.

Don't worry about overfeeding your baby; it is very difficult to overfeed a breastfed baby. Your baby will regulate how much she wants. Under-

When feeding your baby make sure that her nose is not pressed too tightly against your breast. If this happens your baby will not be able to breathe and will stop feeding. Also, make sure that your nipple is in far enough so that the baby can suck on it and create a vacuum with her mouth.

Never pull your baby off the breast. Loosen her mouth by pressing gently but firmly on her chin or slip your finger down between the areola and your baby's cheek and put your little finger into the corner of her mouth. This will make her mouth open and the breast slip out.

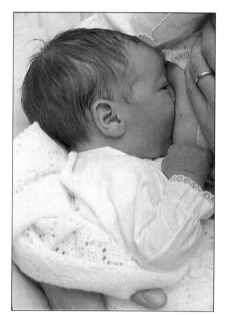

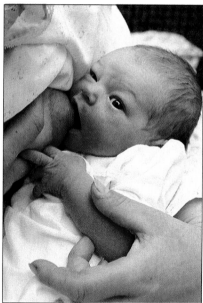

feeding, too, is highly unlikely, though possible. The first sign will probably be that the baby is still sucking even though she has finished feeding from both breasts. Sucking doesn't always signify hunger. It could be thirst or just that your baby likes the comfort of sucking.

BOTTLE FEEDING

Babies thrive and are perfectly happy being bottle fed. Bottle feeding allows your partner to be more involved in the feeding process, and shared feeding schedules can be worked out to give you more rest and unbroken sleep. Babies that are bottle fed sleep longer between feedings during the first few weeks, which also gives you more time to catch up on your rest. Your doctor may advise you to bottle feed if you are taking medication that will be secreted in the breast milk, or if your baby has a physical abnormality, such as a cleft palate, that prevents breastfeeding.

If you are not breastfeeding and cannot give your baby colostrum, your baby will be given some sugared water four to eight hours after delivery and then formula feed after about 48 hours. You will be helped by the medical staff, who will organize the feedings with you. Your baby may not take in all of her first meals, as it takes a while for newborns to get used to feeding. A bottle-fed baby will emit the same signs and signals of hunger as a breastfed baby, and the same signs of being finished with the food.

Bottle-fed babies tend to feed less frequently than breastfed ones. This is because formula milk takes longer to digest; it also contains slightly more protein that provides more calories and, therefore, delays hunger for longer. After the first two or three days, your baby will probably settle into a four-hourly regime taking about two ounces in each bottle. As the amount she takes increases, the number of feedings will decrease.

Buy your feeding equipment before you go into the hospital to have the baby. That way it will all be there when you come home. It also gives you the opportunity to practice in advance, and to develop your routine for cleansing, sterilizing and preparing the formula. I failed to do this with my first baby and I returned home from the hospital with a very hungry and angry baby. It took my husband and I 40 minutes, with the two of us working flat out, to get that newborn baby his food. Don't make our mistake, practice before you have your baby.

When bottle feeding make sure your baby has the same attention and closeness at feeding times as she would have if you were breastfeeding. Make sure you have a quiet, comfortable place to sit and that your arms are well supported with cushions or pillows, if necessary. Lay the baby in your lap with her head in the crook of your elbow and her back supported along your forearm. Gently stroke your baby's cheek to encourage her to take the bottle. Insert the nipple well back into her mouth, making certain it is full of milk.

When you are home, prepare one large supply of formula and store it in bottles in the refrigerator. A bottle-fed baby takes about seven feeds in 24 hours, and this ensures you always have a supply. Bring a bottle out of the refrigerator and allow it to come to room temperature. If you want to warm it a little more, hold it under hot running water or leave it in a bowl of hot water for a few minutes. Never leave the food sitting for even half an hour, as this encourages bacterial growth. When cleaning nipples, push water through the hole to release any old milk.

Make sure the room where you are feeding is quiet and comfortable for both you and the baby, and that your arms are well supported with cushions and pillows if necessary. Hold your baby in your lap with her head in the crook of your elbow and her back supported along your forearm. Don't have your baby lying flat as it makes it difficult for her to swallow and she may gag so use a cushion up against your arm to support her back and keep her head fairly high. Choose your feeding chair, a

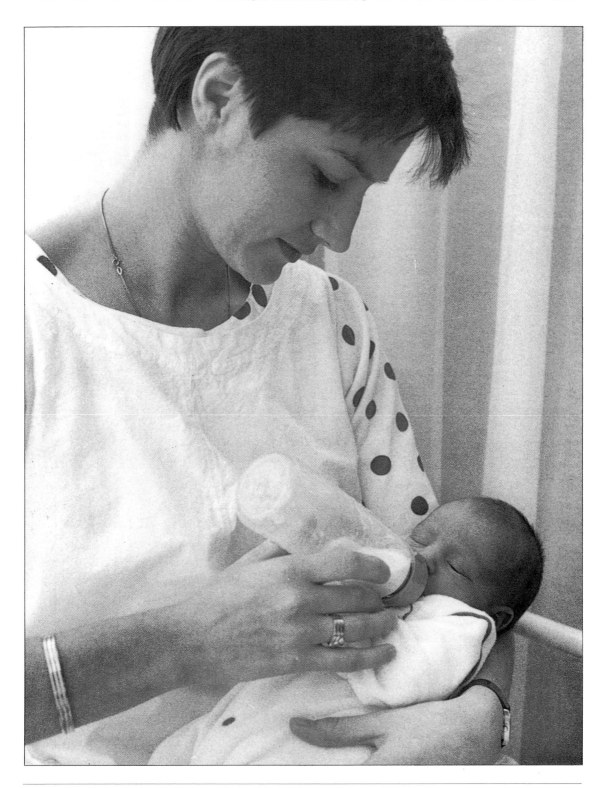

RIGHT
Make feeding times as pleasant as possible. Face your baby and make eye contact. Don't sit in silence; talk, sing, chatter or make any kind of sound you like as long as you sound pleasant, happy and responsive.

BELOW
If you cannot breastfeed your baby, you can still establish contact and bonding during bottle feeding. Special care babies will need to be bottle fed and you should do this yourself as much as possible to establish closeness and allow your baby to become familiar with your touch.

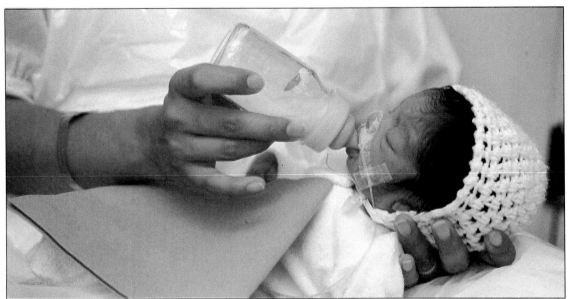

BABY ANDREW

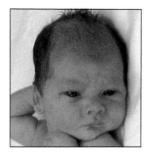

Born: on expected date of delivery

Weight: 7lb 3oz (3250g)

Condition: was in some distress upon birth, fine almost immediately after

Mother's labor: extremely short, lasting 1 hour 40 minutes

Feeding: bottle fed

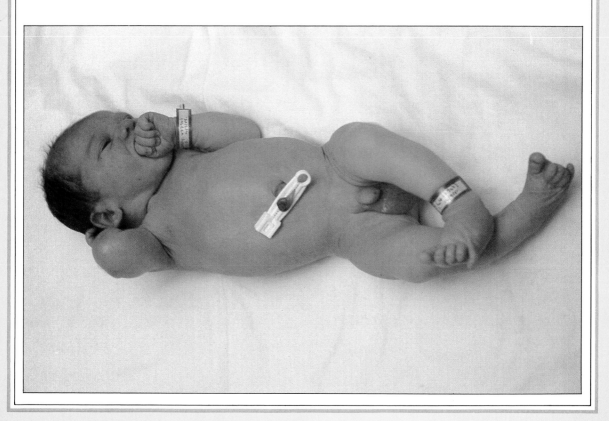

THE FIRST DAY

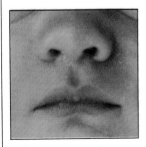

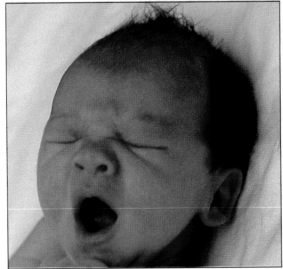

"I noticed his ears were curled up right against his head. When I touched them they opened just like petals".

"He sucked his thumb a couple of hours after he was born".

"We didn't know what I was expecting but we were both very happy he was a boy. He looked just like my husband when he was born".

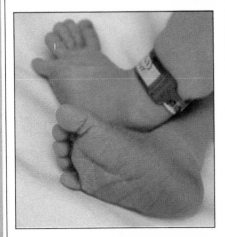

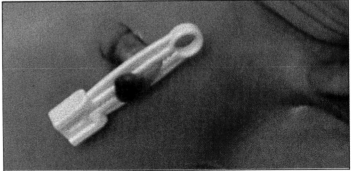

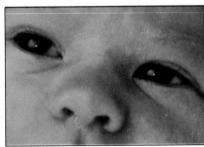

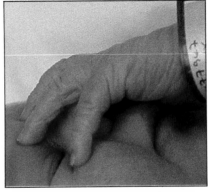

"His hands and feet were very dry and wrinkly and his head had some bumps and parts of it were sunken in. His nails were quite sharp and I had to put baby mitts on him to keep him from scratching himself further".

THE TENTH DAY

" He was born with a lot of dark, thick hair and this got lighter over the next few weeks".

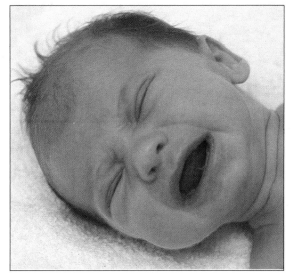

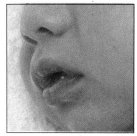

"I was surprised at how alert he was right from the beginning".

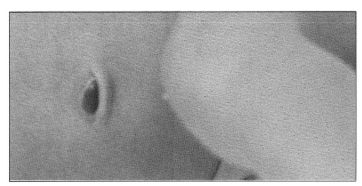

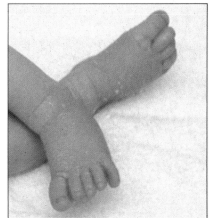

"He didn't gain weight very quickly. He was down to 6lb 10oz when I left the hospital after 5 days. At his 3-week check-up, he was up to 7lb 9oz".

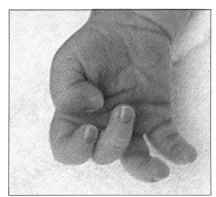

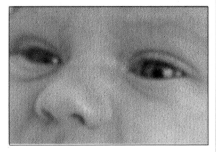

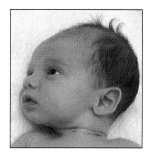

"He is a very pleasant and settled baby. He was that
way in the hospital and has been even more placid since
he has been home. So far he hasn't given me any reason
to panic since he's so good. It makes taking care of him
easy. However, when I was in hospital, I wasn't feeding
him correctly. I held the bottle so tight against his nose
that it became very red".

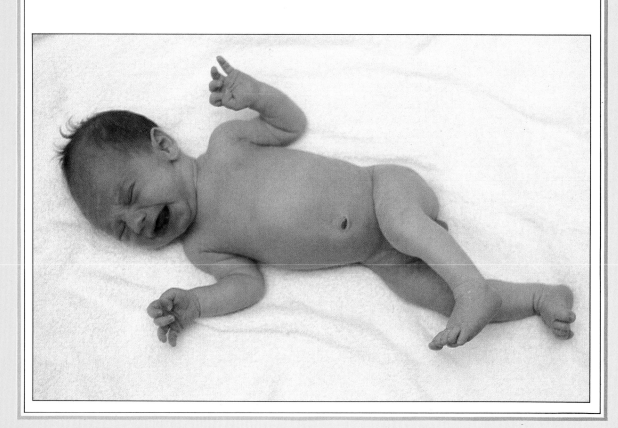

Expressing milk (removing it with a pump device) allows you to use breast milk in your baby's bottle. You may also decide to express your milk if you are bottle feeding as it helps reduce pressure in the breasts and inhibits milk flow. Your nurse will help you to express milk while in the hospital and explain how you can do it at home.

Special care babies often need to be drip fed (through a tube running down their throats into their stomachs) for a few days until they can bottle or breastfeed. If you have expressed milk it may then be used.

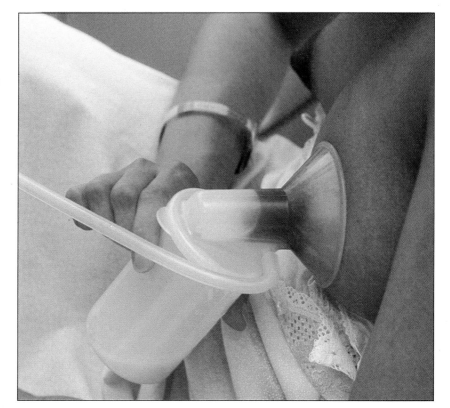

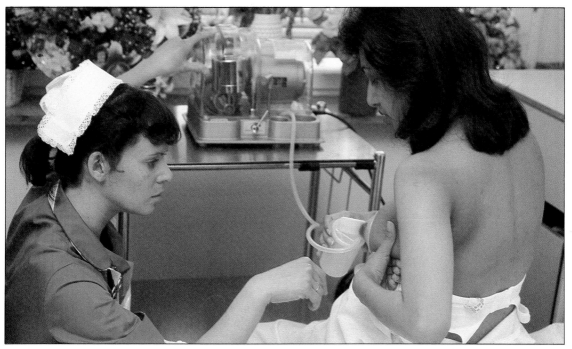

comfortable easy chair that is quite low on the ground is all that is necessary, before you go in to the hospital and put it in the baby's room. Also make sure that everything you need for feeding and changing is within easy reach of where you sit.

Fill the bottle to one ounce more than her largest feeding. Test the heat of the milk by letting a couple of drop fall on to the inside of your wrist. It should be neither hot nor cold to the touch. To elicit your baby's sucking reflex, gently stroke the cheek nearest to you. As she turns, you can gently insert the nipple into her mouth. Make sure the tip is far enough back that she can get good suction, but not so far back that she gags.

It is very important to test that the milk is flowing easily from the nipple of the bottle. Nipples are available with different-sized holes, and there's a size for newborns. Always use the correct-sized nipple; if the hole is too large, the baby will choke and may vomit.

Let your baby set the pace of the feeding. As with breastfeeding, this is a good time to sing, croon or talk to your baby in a soothing voice. Make eye contact during the meal and be sure to face the baby. About halfway through the feeding change arms. This gives your baby something new to look at and gives your arm a rest. You may also want to burp your baby at this point.

Hold the bottle at a downwards angle to make sure that the nipple is always full of milk. This prevents your baby from swallowing air with the food. Usually babies spit out the nipples when they are finished feeding but if you have to remove the bottle, just pull the nipple gently but firmly and your baby should release the bottle. If she doesn't, gently slide yor little finger into the corner of her mouth to break the suction. Don't force your baby to finish the bottle if she indicates that she's had enough.

BURPING

Your baby will possibly suck in air with her feed. The amount of air that babies suck in varies. Bottle-fed babies tend to swallow more than breastfed ones, but this doesn't necessarily mean it will be a problem.

Most baby books over-estimate the amount of discomfort caused by gas and over-emphasize the necessity for burping your baby. There is no research on babies that shows burping makes them any more restful, comforted and docile. However, it is a good opportunity to take a breather in the middle and at the end of a meal, to hold your baby upright so she looks around, and for you to give the baby a little gentle cuddle and a massage on her back. This is good for both of you. Burping in the middle of a feeding is also recommended because air takes up room in the stomach. If your baby burps, she will eat the right amount of food. But don't keep your baby up there a protracted time until she's burped; it's quite unnecessary.

To burp your baby, hold her upright against your chest and gently pat or rub her back. Don't pat or rub too hard, as you may jerk your baby and cause her to bring up the food. A gentle upward stroking movement is usually preferable to firm pats. This slight movement releases the air in her stomach. If she is held upright no milk will come up with the air.

Don't lay your baby straight into her crib without burping; she may bring up part of her meal or the gas will pass into her intestine where it may cause discomfort and colicky pain.

If you like, you can burp your baby either in the middle or at the end of a feed. Hold your baby over your shoulder, sit her on your knee with her chin well supported, or lay your baby on your lap with her face down.

Don't pat or rub your baby too hard. You may jerk your baby and she will bring up some of the food. Use gentle, upward stroking movements instead. Gently rub or pat your baby's back between her shoulder blades.

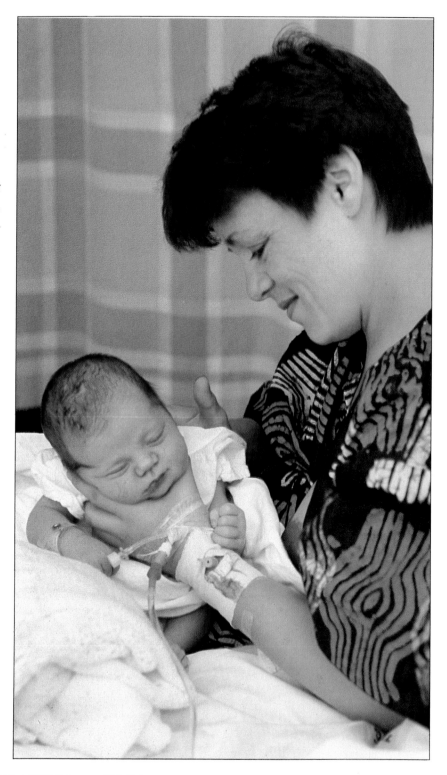

FEEDING

You can feed your baby in whatever position you choose as long as you are comfortable and relaxed. For breastfeeding mothers it is essential, too, that the position enables your baby to fix on the nipple. Experiment and use whichever position feels most natural. If you are going to sit down and feed your baby, make sure that you are in a comfortable position, with your arms and back supported with cushions or pillows, if necessary. It is also quite nice to lie in bed to feed your baby, especially in the first few weeks and at night. Lie on your side, propped with pillows if that is more comfortable, and gently cradle the baby alongside you. If you are bottle feeding, make certain your baby is not lying horizontally while she feeds. She should be half sitting so that breathing and swallowing are both safe and easy and there is no risk of her choking. When your baby has finished feeding, remove her gently from your breast, or the bottle from her, breaking any suction.

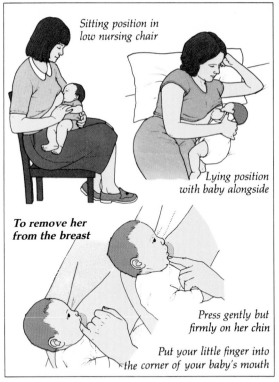

Sitting position in low nursing chair

Lying position with baby alongside

To remove her from the breast

Press gently but firmly on her chin

Put your little finger into the corner of your baby's mouth

WARMING THE BOTTLE

Allow milk to come to room temperature by letting it stand or run hot water on it to heat it quickly.

Or, stand the bottle in hot water. Test the temperature on your wrist before feeding.

CHECKING THE FLOW OF MILK

Invert the feeding bottle. If the milk comes out in a gush the hole is too big. If the drops of milk come out in a steady stream, the hole is correct. If it takes a few seconds for a drop to form, the hole is too small.

REMOVING A BOTTLE

Prevent your baby swallowing air by holding the bottle so that the nipple is full of milk.

When the feed is finished, and before she can suck in any air, pull the nipple gently but firmly and she should release the bottle.

If she doesn't release the bottle, gently slide your little finger into the corner of her mouth. This will break any suction, but is usually not necessary.

HOLDING AND HANDLING

Although your newborn may seem very vulnerable, she is really quite robust. But, in the early weeks, the sensation of being tightly enclosed gives a great sense of security. You should hold your baby firmly and, when you move her, do it as slowly, gently, and as quietly as you possibly can. Never shake your baby or handle her roughly.

Until she is about four weeks old, your baby will have little control over her lolling head because her neck muscles are not strong enough to support it. You must, therefore, always support her head when holding her. When carrying her either cradle her in the crook of an arm or hold her against the upper part of your chest.

Picking up your baby

Slide one hand under her neck to support the head. Slide the other underneath her back and bottom to support her lower half

Pick her up gently and smoothly and transfer her to a carrying position

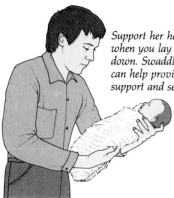

Support her head when you lay her down. Swaddling can help provide support and security

Hold your baby so that her head is slightly higher than her body

Use your forearm to cradle your baby against your chest, holding her head with your free hand

USING A SHAWL AS A SLING

Drape the shawl around your shoulders, with a slightly shorter length on the side where you will hold the baby.

Holding her in the crook of your arm, fold the shorter edge over her body, leaving her feet free. Wrap the fabric securely.

Bring the other length of fabric over and under your baby, then pull the fabric up between your chest and the baby.

Tuck the remaining fabric neatly inside the "pocket" you have just folded. The shawl will leave you with both hands free if you wish.

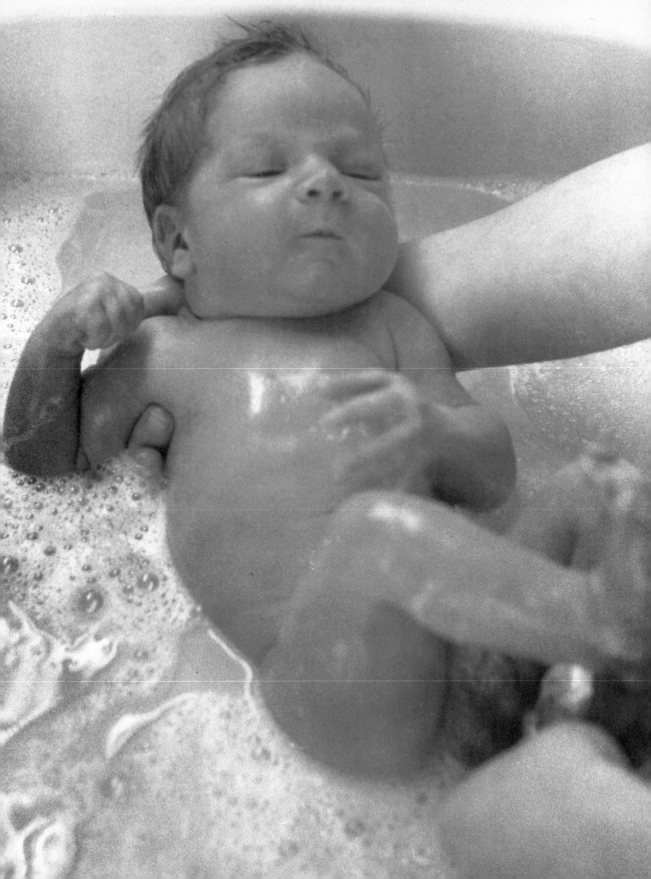

6
TAKING CARE OF YOUR BABY

Parents are made, not born, and most people today learn about taking care of babies by having one. Don't expect to be an expert right away; everyone needs time and practice before they can change and dress a baby without feeling flustered.

During the first few weeks of life, your main preoccupations will be to feed, dress and change your baby and to see that he sleeps. You will also clean your baby, though giving him a bath every day is not necessary, and care for his navel. These tasks don't appear to be onerous but, in fact, you may be feeding him up to ten times a day and changing him at least as frequently, if not more.

Newborn babies are awake for up to nine hours out of every 24, and you should make the most of them. For the baby, the single greatest aspect of care is feeding; for the both of you it is bonding — that is, creating a relationship that is unique between the two of you.

Parenting is a shared task. While caring for a baby can appear to be a series of repetitive chores, it is really the best way for you, your partner, and your baby to discover what it is to be a family.

Babies love body contact and being held. When you cuddle your baby, talk and sing softly to him, and kiss and touch him as much as possible. This helps to make your baby feel secure, and also helps him recognize your feel, smell and sound.

When you talk and sing to him, look into his eyes. This helps to establish contact and your baby will soon be able to recognize the shape of your face.

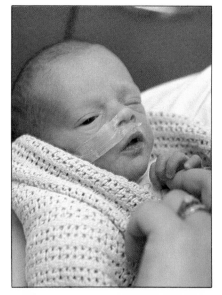

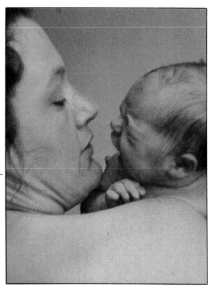

BONDING

Bonding is nature's way of ensuring that children are nurtured and that the human race, as a whole, survives. Through the process of getting to know your baby intimately, you will stimulate strong feelings of attachment, protectiveness and possessiveness that will fashion a relationship that is probably the strongest you will ever experience.

Establishing a relationship with your baby begins the second he is born. If possible, you should be left in private with a minimum of interruption. Babies are responsive to a nurturing adult as soon as they are born, and while it has been shown that the first 35 to 45 minutes are the most rewarding for getting to know your baby through eye-to-eye and skin-to-

It is particularly important to make the baby's father feel as involved as possible during the first few days when much of the attention is on you and your new baby. Babies soon learn to recognize their fathers, from the sound of their voices, their appearances and their touch. Many babies are soothed by the low-pitched sounds men make, and your partner should talk and sing to your baby as much as possible.

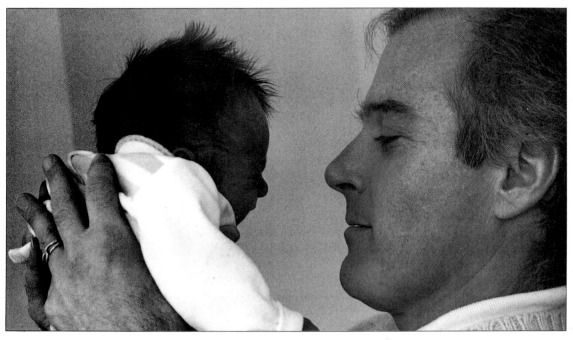

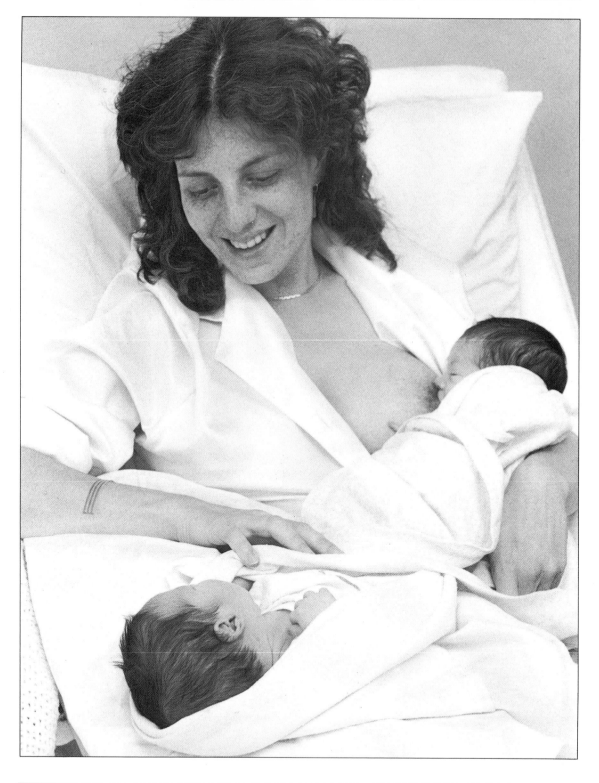

skin contact, the bonding process is an ongoing one.

Although immediately after birth the baby is usually very awake, he is very sleepy for the next 24 hours and may not even be interested in feeding. Therefore, try to spend as much of his waking time with him as possible. Research has shown that physical contact, the sound of your voice, your smell, touch, and the feel of your skin is very important in the first days for your baby to form a bond with you.

The first thing about you that your baby recognizes is your smell and then your voice. All of us secrete a special hormone called a pheromone through our skins which has a very strong smell. We are most sensitive to it during our first days and weeks of life. Subsequently, we tend to lose sensitivity to that smell but in newborn babies it performs a very useful function. Because they are so sensitive to it, they can distinguish your smell from everybody else's, which is why, when you go into the baby's room, he will wake immediately whereas he will remain sound asleep if anyone else enters the room. He wakes because he can sniff you on the air.

After smell, your baby is most sensitive to your voice; this is why you should start talking to your baby from the minute he is born and never stop; whatever you are doing, keep up a running commentary and whenever you do anything for him, keep your face that important 8–10 inches away and chatter. Your smell and the sound of your voice make your baby feel calm and secure so use a soft, gentle, soothing voice and whenever possible, sing or croon to your baby.

Facial expression, tone of voice and response to his needs, such as feeding, changing, holding, are ways of showing love. Babies want love all the time.

You will probably find it easier to love your baby if he is responsive to you, feeds easily and happily, and does not cry excessively. However, to most mothers, their babies seem to be more difficult than they ever expected, so don't be surprised if you become anxious at a time when you are less able to tolerate such feelings, and you may even become resentful of what you might interpret as the baby's refusal to cooperate. It is important that you approach the situation with your sense of humor intact. After all, you have as much experience of being a mother as he has of being an independent being. You may not always interpret his needs correctly, and his only response, therefore, may be to cry.

After some time spent with his parents, a baby born by cesarean is often routinely whisked away to the nursery for special observation and care if it is suspected he may have respiratory difficulties. If he is in good condition there is, of course, no reason why he can't be with you. But if he is taken away for some time, then he will need extra loving and cuddling. If you find it difficult getting up to see him, ask the nursing staff that he be brought to you. Twins, because they are usually of a lower birth weight, also may need to be put in a special care unit for a while as will premature babies. If your baby is in a separate nursery and even if he has to be cared for in an incubator, you should insist on being allowed to visit him as often as possible. Through the portholes in the incubator you can touch and caress him and perhaps feed him as well. It is important to take all the measures you can to reduce the amount of time you are apart.

Usually, special care babies can be held and cuddled in the unit unless there is a risk of infection. You may find it distressing that you cannot have your baby with you all the time, but many special care babies can be taken out of their incubators during feeding, for instance.

Many incubators in these wards have openings for your hands so that you can touch and fondle your baby without needing to remove him from the temperature-regulated environment. This allows you to bond with your baby and develop the necessary closeness.

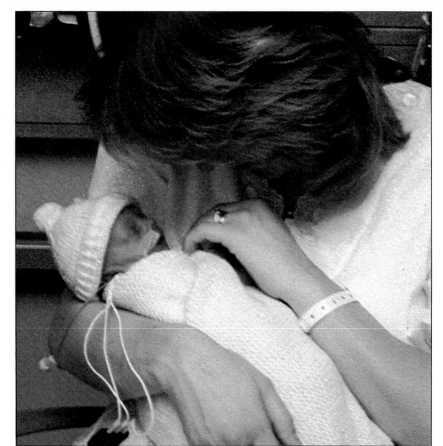

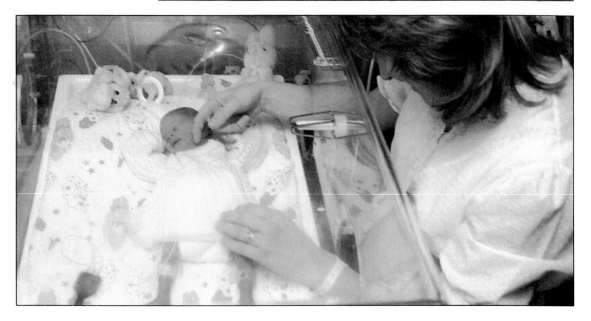

Premature and special care babies are cared for in separate wards where full-time nursing care and special monitoring equipment is available. It may be harder for you to bond with your baby if he is in a special care ward, so you should try to make an effort to spend as much time there with him as possible.

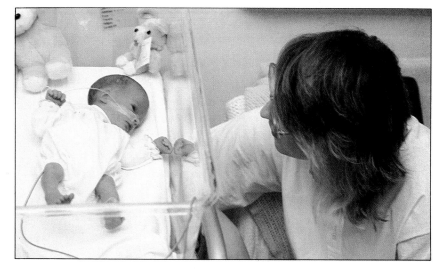

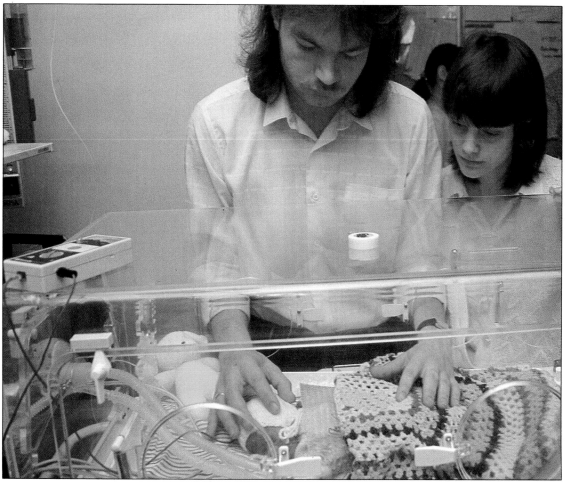

HOLDING YOUR BABY

From the time that he's born up until about three months, your baby really likes a firm hold so that he feels safe and secure. Although your newborn baby seems very vulnerable he is not breakable. Do not be scared of holding him. He is quite robust and has enough muscle control except for his head.

Hold your baby close to you, talk soothingly and lovingly as you look into his eyes. Hold your baby firmly, especially in the early weeks when the sensation of being tightly enclosed gives a great sense of security. This is why the old-fashioned idea of swaddling or tightly wrapping your baby in a shawl did work (though it's not necessarily healthy for your baby as it restricts movement). It works because the baby feels tightly bound as it did inside your womb for six or seven months. When moving your baby, do it slowly, gently and as quietly as possible. Do not shake him.

When picking up your baby, take care of his lolling head. Your baby won't have good muscle control around the head and will need to have it supported until he is about four weeks old. Always pick him up in a way that supports his head. To do this, slide one hand under your baby's neck to support the head. Slide your other hand underneath your baby's back and

When you hold your baby you should always support his head securely. Although many of your baby's muscles are well developed, those in his neck cannot support the weight of his head. It will be a few months before your baby will be able to hold his head up all by himself.

Hold your baby as much as possible. You may have your baby rooming in with you, which means you can spend as much time as possible with him. This helps you to get to know your baby and to learn to understand his sounds, movements and cries.

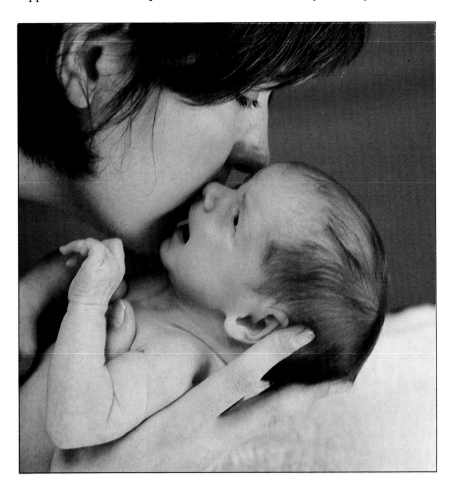

bottom to support the lower half securely. Held this way, your baby can easily be transferred to any of the carrying positions.

When laying down your baby, again make sure his head is supported. If you don't, his head may fall back and flop. Put down your baby in the way suggested for picking him up, or use your whole arm to support the spine, neck and head, or alternatively wrap your baby tightly in a shawl so his head is supported until he is down and you can unwrap the shawl.

There are two main positions for carrying your newborn baby. You can hold him in the crook of either arm, with his head slightly higher than the rest of his body, which rests on the upper part of your arm and is encircled by your forearm and hand which supports his back and bottom. This is a good position to hold and carry a baby because it allows eye contact and you can talk and smile at your baby.

The second way is to hold your baby against the upper part of your chest, using your forearm, with his head resting on your shoulder supported by your hand. This leaves one hand free, which is essential if you are alone and need to pick something up.

DIAPERS

Your baby will go through a lot of diapers. Diapers are now produced in a wide variety of styles and sizes, but the basic choice is between disposable and fabric.

Disposable diapers have the advantage of convenience, and there is no washing or drying. The cost can mount up, however. They are easier to put on a baby as there is no elaborate folding, diaper pins or waterproof pants. They are usually secured with adjustable adhesive tabs. Choose disposables that are free of dioxins or unbleached.

Cloth diapers are much more absorbent, but must be washed and dried after every use. If you choose fabric diapers, you should plan on having at least two dozen good ones. They are made of terrycloth, gauze, bird's-eye and flannel and again come in a variety of styles and sizes. They have to be washed, rinsed, sterilized, and dried after every use. Terrycloth diapers can be very bulky on newborn babies, so you should have some gauze ones on hand for the first few weeks. They are soft and filmy and feel soft against your baby's skin. They are not as absorbent as terrycloth diapers and need to be changed frequently.

Diaper liners are placed inside the diaper and go next to the baby's skin. The best variety is made of a special material which lets urine pass through but remains dry next to the baby's skin. Liners minimize the risk of a sore bottom due to friction or moisture. They also catch most of the feces and prevent the diaper from getting badly soiled.

Waterproof pants are useful with cloth diapers but they promote diaper rash because they keep the diaper area wetter and warmer. You can use them if your baby's skin is clear but leave them off if he has a rash. You will need about six pairs.

When putting on diapers, make sure everything you need is close at hand and within easy reach. I think it is a good idea to set up a permanent changing area which you can easily keep clean and tidy, where everything is within arm's reach. In addition to clean diapers you will need baby lotion or oil, tissues, cottonballs, baby wipes, a washcloth, water, diaper rash

DIAPER CHANGING

It is a good idea to establish a permanent diaper changing corner in the baby's room where you can have all the supplies ready. You will also need to take diapers and wipes with you when you take the baby out. Today, diaper bags that unfold and allow you to change the baby on any flat surface, disposable diapers, and baby wipes make changing your baby easy to manage.

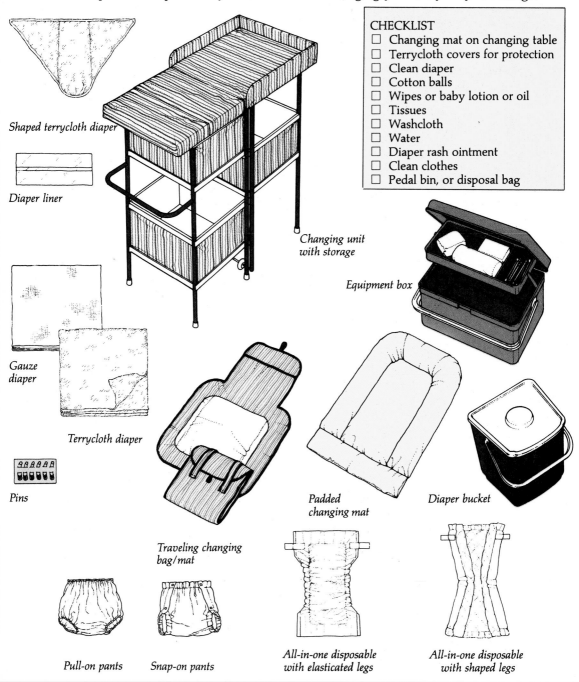

CHECKLIST
- ☐ Changing mat on changing table
- ☐ Terrycloth covers for protection
- ☐ Clean diaper
- ☐ Cotton balls
- ☐ Wipes or baby lotion or oil
- ☐ Tissues
- ☐ Washcloth
- ☐ Water
- ☐ Diaper rash ointment
- ☐ Clean clothes
- ☐ Pedal bin, or disposal bag

Shaped terrycloth diaper

Diaper liner

Changing unit with storage

Equipment box

Gauze diaper

Terrycloth diaper

Pins

Padded changing mat

Diaper bucket

Traveling changing bag/mat

Pull-on pants

Snap-on pants

All-in-one disposable with elasticated legs

All-in-one disposable with shaped legs

CLEANING A BOY

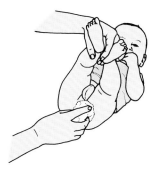

If the diaper is soiled, remove feces with any clean parts of the diaper. Using one cotton ball with lotion or oil, or one baby wipe at a time, remove the rest. Clean your hands.

Using a wet cloth, cotton ball or a baby wipe, remove urine working from the leg creases in towards the penis. Don't pull the foreskin back.

Lift up his legs, holding both ankles in one hand with your finger in-between his heels. Using another part of the cloth or new cotton ball or wipe, clean his bottom. Dry thoroughly.

CLEANING A GIRL

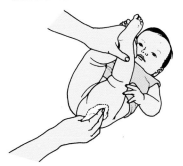

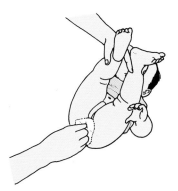

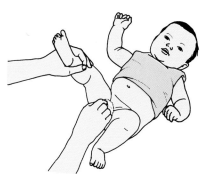

If the diaper is soiled, remove feces with any clean parts of the diaper. Using one cotton ball with lotion or oil, or one baby wipe at a time, remove the rest. Clean your hands.

Using a wet cloth, cotton ball or a baby wipe, remove urine from the vulva and the surrounding skin, including the leg creases. Never pull back the labia to clean inside.

Holding both ankles in one hand clean her bottom. Wipe from the vagina back towards the rectum using part of the cloth, a new cotton ball or wipe. Never wipe from back to front.

PUTTING ON AN ALL-IN-ONE DISPOSABLE DIAPER

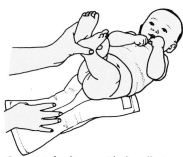

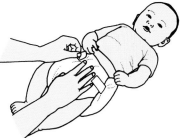

Open out the diaper with the adhesive tabs at the top. Lay the baby on top of the diaper, or slide the diaper under, so that the top aligns with the baby's waist at the back.

Bring the front of the diaper up between the baby's legs. If the top of the diaper isn't elasticated, tuck the thinner edge in over the top padding across the tummy.

Unpeel the adhesive and pull the tabs firmly over to secure the diaper. If necessary tuck sides in around the thighs. If the umbilical cord is still present, fold the top back.

CLOTH DIAPERS

Though initially more expensive to buy than all-in-one disposables, cloth diapers work out cheaper over the years and some mothers prefer the softness of gauze next to their babies' skins. Made of terrycloth, gauze or bird's-eye, they have to be rinsed, sterilized, washed out, and dried after use. Buy a minimum of 24 diapers. You will also need to have 12 diaper pins, which are specially designed with self-locking heads. Although you may not use them right away, you will need at least 6 pairs of waterproof pants when your baby is older. Diaper liners, which are placed inside the diaper next to the baby's skin, allow urine to pass through but keep the baby's skin drier, thus minimizing the risk of a sore bottom. They also catch most of the feces and prevent the diaper from getting badly soiled.

CHECKLIST	
☐ Cloth diaper	☐ Water
☐ 2 diaper pins	☐ Diaper rash ointment,
☐ Diaper liner	if necessary
☐ Cotton balls	☐ Clean clothes
☐ Wipes or baby	☐ Diaper bucket
lotion or oil	

PUTTING ON A FABRIC DIAPER

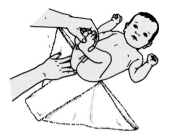 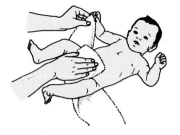 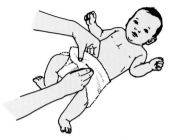

Slide the diaper under your baby so that her waist aligns with the top edge. The triple absorbent fold is the most absorbent and neatest for a newborn.

Bring the diaper up between her legs. Hold it in place and first fold one side over the central panel and then the other side.

For a small baby, secure the diaper with one pin in the middle of the panel; for a larger baby, use two side pins.

TRIPLE ABSORBENT FOLD METHOD

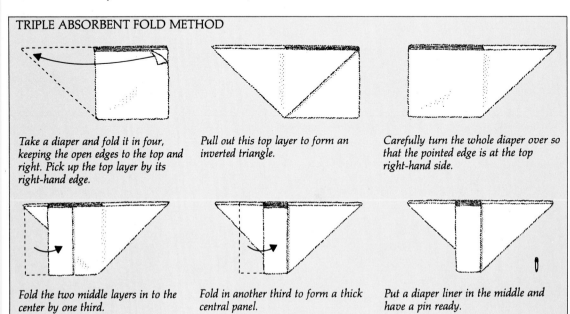

Take a diaper and fold it in four, keeping the open edges to the top and right. Pick up the top layer by its right-hand edge.

Pull out this top layer to form an inverted triangle.

Carefully turn the whole diaper over so that the pointed edge is at the top right-hand side.

Fold the two middle layers in to the center by one third.

Fold in another third to form a thick central panel.

Put a diaper liner in the middle and have a pin ready.

TOPPING AND TAILING

Most newborns don't need cleaning very often because except for their bottoms, faces, necks and skin creases they rarely get dirty. Since you will only have to give him a bath every 2 or 3 days, this method allows you to wash the parts that really need it, and cause the minimum of disturbance and distress. If the water supply is suspect, use boiled water in place of warm tap water.

CHECKLIST
- [ ] Warm water
- [ ] Baby lotion or oil or baby wipes
- [ ] Cotton balls
- [ ] Towel
- [ ] Washcloth
- [ ] Clean diaper
- [ ] Diaper liner
- [ ] Pins and waterproof pants, if used
- [ ] Clean clothes

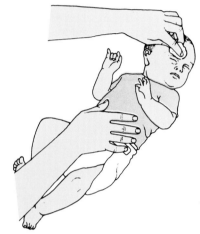

Lay your baby on a firm surface. Taking a moist cotton ball for each eye, gently wipe from the bridge of the nose outwards.

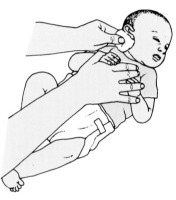

Wipe outside and behind his ears with a cotton ball. Do not poke about or clean inside them.

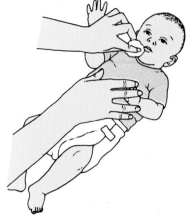

Wipe your baby's face with a damp cotton ball to remove any milk or drool. If left, this will irritate the baby's skin.

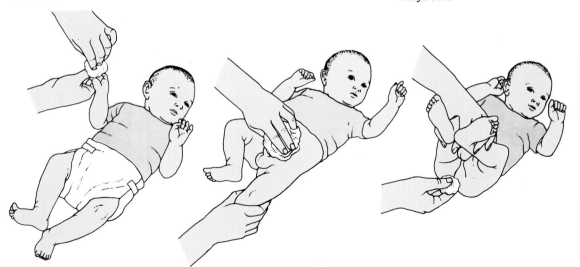

Use a new cotton ball and clear water to clean your baby's hands. Dry with a towel. (When your baby is older you can use a washcloth.)

Take off his old diaper. If he is just wet, wipe the area with a washcloth or a damp cotton ball.

If he is soiled, remove as much as you can with the diaper, then use baby lotion and cotton balls or baby wipes to clean the diaper area.

121

ointment, if necessary, cornstarch baby powder, a pedal bin and a distracting toy.

Begin by removing the dirty diaper. Use the front of it to clear any feces off your baby. Fold the dirty diaper so that the feces can't fall out and place it to one side of the changing mat. Then clean your baby's genital area. With a boy, work from the leg creases towards the penis; with a girl, wipe from the vagina back towards the rectum. Next, clean the top of the legs and then, holding both ankles in one hand, clean the buttocks. There is no need to wash your baby's bottom with soap at each change. It is usually sufficient to wipe away most of the feces using wipes or plain water and a cotton ball. When he is clean, put on a fresh diaper. Put your baby down somewhere safe before disposing of the diaper and washing your hands. Never leave your baby on a changing table.

Change a diaper whenever you notice that it is soiled or wet. This could be very often with newborns, as they urinate frequently. The number of changes will vary from day to day and baby to baby. However, you will probably need to change the diaper when your baby wakes, when he is put to bed and after every feed, due to the reflex that stimulates elimination when food is taken in. Don't change your baby before feeding, he's hungry and it will only make him irritable, added to which most babies pass a stool during or after their feed so you will be doubling up on your work.

DIAPER RASHES

Diaper rash is probably the most common condition affecting healthy babies. A substance called urea, always present in the urine, is turned into ammonia by bacteria that are normally found on babies' skin which contaminate wet or soiled diapers. Ammonia irritates the skin, causing diaper rash where it has been in contact with the skin for any length of time. Diaper rash can range from mild redness and soreness to an inflamed area of broken skin. Bottle-fed babies are more prone to diaper rash, as bacteria thrives in an alkaline medium, which is what the stools of bottle-fed babies are. To minimize the possibility of diaper rash:

● Try to use unbleached disposable diapers. Some diapers are made using a bleaching process that releases toxic dioxins.
● Change diapers regularly; never leave your baby lying in a wet diaper.
● If you are using a cloth diaper, put a one-way disposable liner next to your baby's skin. This allows urine to pass straight through to be absorbed by the diaper below, and so keeps the skin dry.
● Keep your baby's bottom clean and dry.
● Leave the baby's bottom open to the air whenever you can.
● Make sure the diapers are well washed and rinsed to remove all the ammonia.
● Don't wait for the skin to actually break. At the first sign of any reddened or broken skin, start using a special ointment for the prevention of diaper rash. In addition, stop using waterproof pants as they help to keep the urine close to the skin and aid the formation of ammonia.
● Stop washing the baby's bottom with soap and water. They are drying to the skin and can cause it to become more cracked.
● To protect the skin, use only baby lotion or diaper rash ointment; don't use over-the-counter antiseptic creams, which can be irritating.

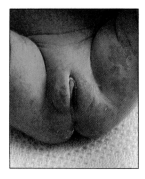

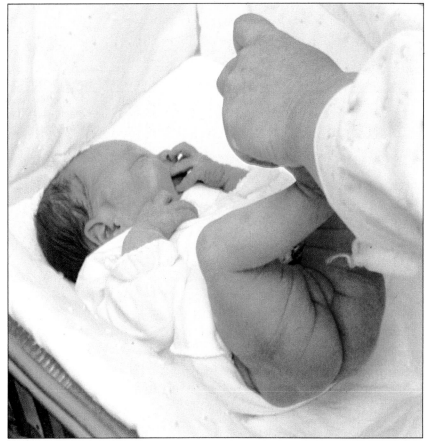

Diaper rash is a very common problem, and it is important to keep the diaper area meticulously clean and dry to prevent it developing. Change the diaper any time it is wet or dirty. Wipe the genital area with the clean corner of the diaper, then with baby lotion, before drying gently. You may find that a barrier cream such as petroleum jelly helps to protect the skin.

If your baby develops diaper rash, keep the skin clean and dry. Do not use powder in the area. You might ask your doctor to provide you with a special ointment or lotion.

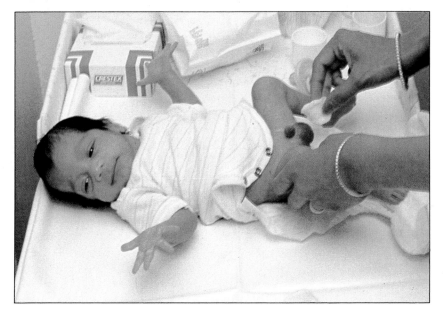

CLOTHING

Babies need changing frequently in the first weeks of life. Don't worry about not being fully confident about holding your baby and dealing with clothes at the same time. You will be a little awkward at first. Always dress and undress your baby by laying him on a flat surface. A changing mat, the bed or the floor are all ideal. Young babies dislike being undressed. The air on their naked bodies may be uncomfortable and the removal of the comforting fabric that they were wearing makes them feel very insecure. Keep the amount of time your baby is undressed to a minimum, cover bare parts with a towel, and don't get flustered if he cries when you take off his clothes. It might help if you do something to attract the baby's attention. All babies like to look at their mothers' faces, so hold yours close. I always used to look at, and talk to my babies constantly while I changed their diapers. If you have a baby boy, when you take the diaper off, don't lean your face too close to him because boys have a habit of peeing and shooting urine right into your face as soon as their diapers are removed.

Babies do not like being dressed and undressed, so make the process as comfortable as possible. You should try to get clothes that have snaps or buttons down the front, as babies dislike having clothes pulled over their faces. Tops that must be pulled over the head can be difficult and awkward to put on.

The type of clothing you need will depend on whether your baby is born during the summer or winter. In winter the clothing should be chosen for warmth, as babies lose a lot of heat. Keep clothing simple: babies know no difference between night and day so you can use stretchy all-in-one garments throughout the 24 hours. It is better to have several thin layers than one thick one. The commonest cause of discomfort and crying is overheating. It's much more important to have the room warm than the baby

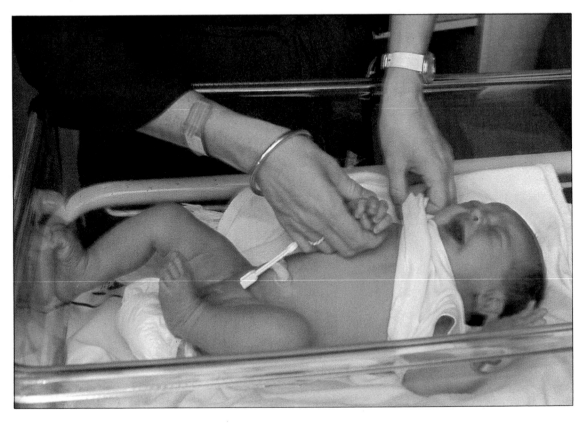

It is a good idea to dress your baby on a flat surface so that both your hands are free to deal with the clothes. Keep the amount of time he is undressed down to a minimum, and do not get flustered if he cries when you take off his clothes. Babies respond to the cooler air on their skins by crying.

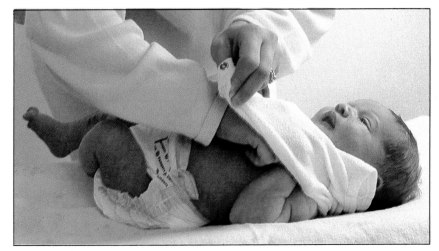

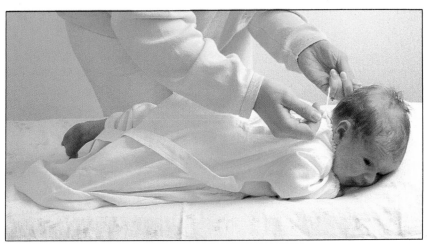

LAYETTE

In the hospital your baby will be provided with all the clothes he needs, but most mothers prefer to buy or borrow a selection of baby clothes ahead of time to have on hand for when they are home. And, of course, your baby will need going-home clothes. Babies need frequent changing and the layette illustrated below should be taken as the minimum. A winter baby needs a few more outer garments than a summer baby. Buy clothes sufficiently large so they will last at least until your baby is two months old. Make certain everything is machine-washable, non-flammable and is of a soft and comfortable material with no hard seams or rough stitching. Choose clothes that open down the front or have wide neck openings. Avoid white — it gets dirty quickly and needs more care when washing — but make sure clothes are color-fast.

CHECKLIST FOR A SUMMER BABY	
☐ 4 lightweight stretch suits	☐ 1 bonnet or summer hat with brim
☐ 4 wide-necked cotton T-shirts or kimono-style undershirts	☐ 2 bibs
☐ 2 drawstring closing nightdresses	☐ 1 box newborn-size disposables or 4 dozen cloth diapers
☐ 2 woolen cardigans	☐ 6 pairs waterproof pants (opt.)
☐ 2 pairs of cotton socks or bootees	☐ 6 diaper pins
☐ 2 receiving blankets	

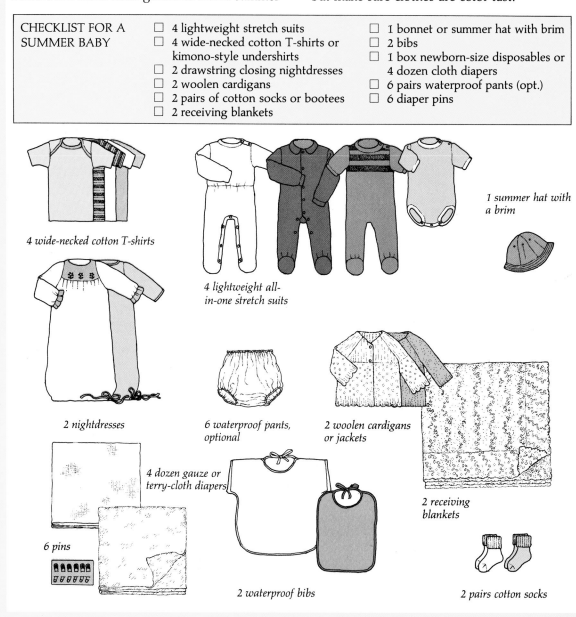

4 wide-necked cotton T-shirts

4 lightweight all-in-one stretch suits

1 summer hat with a brim

2 nightdresses

6 waterproof pants, optional

2 woolen cardigans or jackets

4 dozen gauze or terry-cloth diapers

2 receiving blankets

6 pins

2 waterproof bibs

2 pairs cotton socks

CHECKLIST FOR A WINTER BABY	☐ 4 stretch suits ☐ 4 wide-necked cotton T-shirts or kimono-style undershirts ☐ 2 drawstring closing nightdresses ☐ 2 woolen cardigans ☐ 1 woolen hat ☐ 2 pairs woolen socks or bootees ☐ 2 pairs mittens	☐ 3 receiving blankets ☐ 2 bibs ☐ 1 box newborn-size disposables or 4 dozen cloth diapers ☐ 6 pairs waterproof pants (opt.) ☐ 6 diaper pins ☐ 1 sleeping bag or snow suit (opt.)

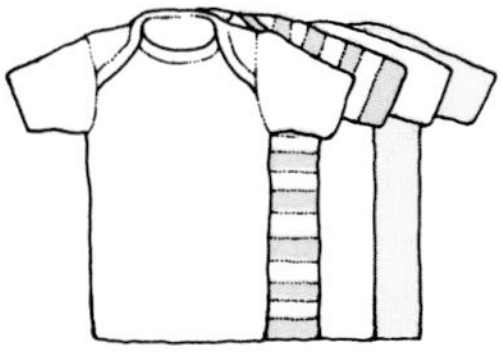

4 wide-necked cotton T-shirts

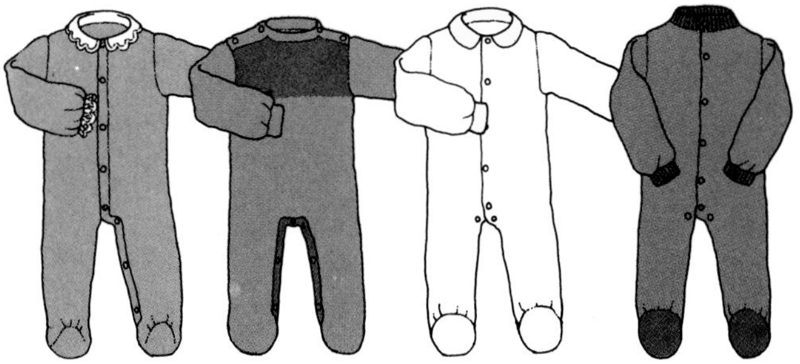

4 all-in-one stretch suits

2 nightdresses

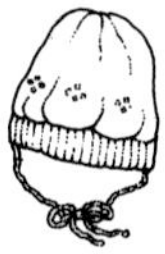

1 woolen hat

2 woolen cardigans or jackets

2 pairs mittens

3 receiving blankets

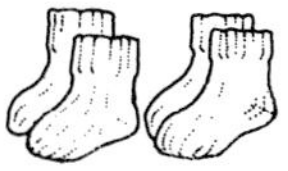

2 pairs woolen socks

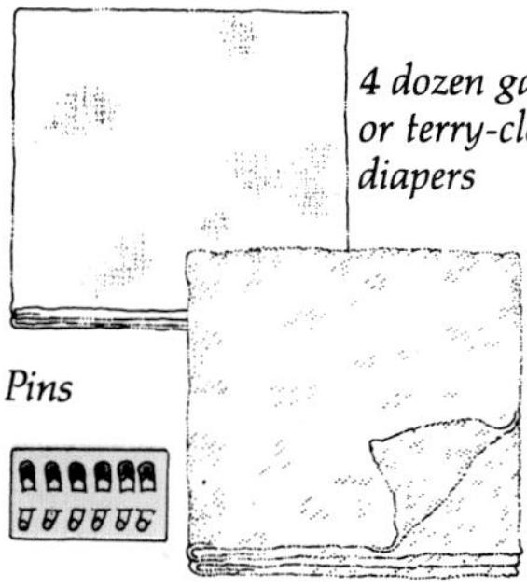

4 dozen gauze or terry-cloth diapers

2 waterproof bibs

Pins

6 waterproof pants, optional

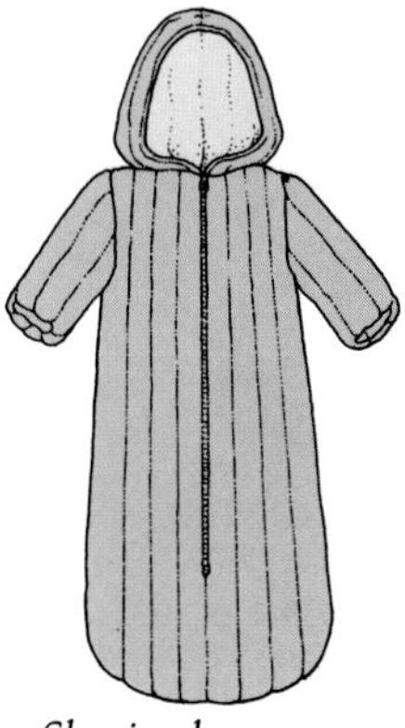

Sleeping bag, optional

Snow suit, optional

smothered with lots of layers of heavy clothing. This also means that you can easily remove layers as the temperature of the room changes. Undershirts may be needed to keep your baby warm or, if it is hot, sometimes all he will need is a top and a diaper.

Choose clothes that have wide necks or that snap or button down the front. Babies seem to dislike having things pulled over their heads and their faces covered. Avoid lacy or delicate fabrics as they can get caught on the baby's fingers or toes. Make sure the material is machine-washable and color-fast. It should be soft and comfortable, with as few seams and rough stitching as possible. Ensure that all clothing is flame-retardant. (See also p. 126 for your layette.)

BATHING

Your newborn baby won't need bathing in a bathtub, because apart from his bottom, face, neck and skin creases, he won't get dirty. The way you should give your newborn baby a bath is in the form of a sponge bath. Hold him in your lap or lay him on a changing mat, have a damp sponge or washcloth on hand, and remove only the minimum amount of clothing at a

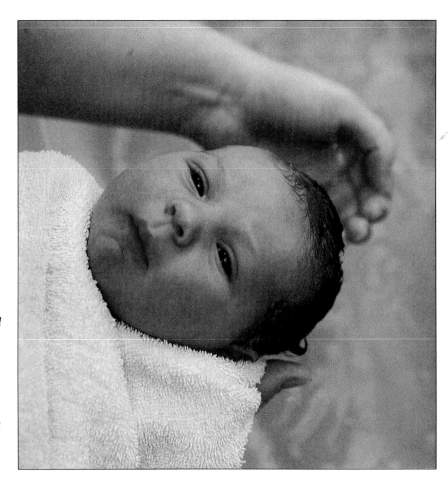

Most newborns do not need baths in the early days and you may prefer just to top and tail, which involves washing just the head, hands and feet. Keep your baby swaddled when washing his head and hair, and hold him with his back firmly supported by your hand. Rinse his hair well and pat dry with a towel.

When you bathe your baby be sure to test the water first to make sure it is not too hot. Keep your baby wrapped up until it is time to place him in the bath, as babies do not like being undressed. Lower your baby into the bath gently, supporting his head and neck and back.

Keep your baby well supported while he is in the bath, and hold him so that he is facing you. Always keep his head and shoulders clear of the water.

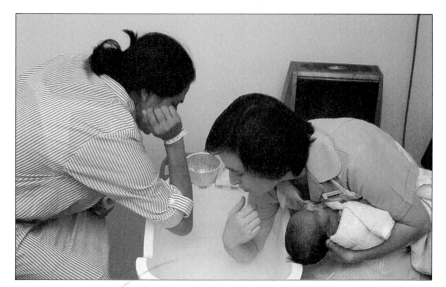

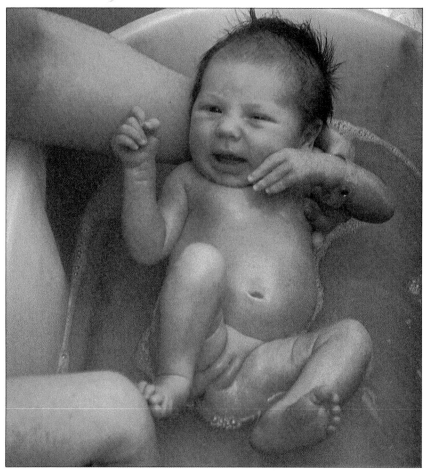

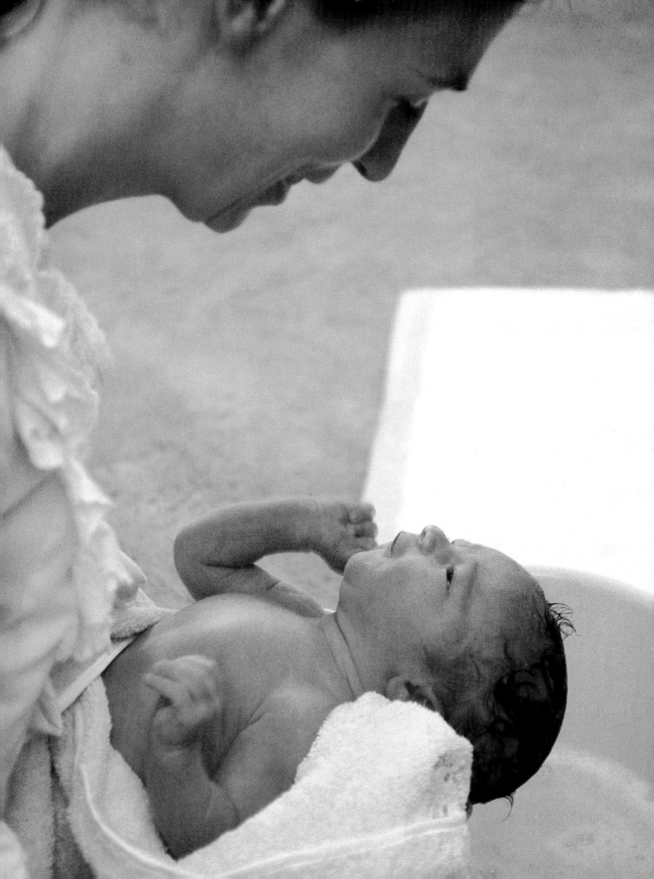

time. Have a lovely, warm soft towel for him to sit and lie on and keep his bare skin covered by the folds of the towel. Clean his face using warm water then go on to do his hands, and finally his genital area. If he's soiled, use his diaper to clean the area as best you can, then use wipes, cotton balls and water to remove any remaining feces, especially in the creases.

It is recommended to give your baby only a sponge bath until the umbilical cord falls off. After this, you can try an actual bath. Fill a baby bath no deeper than 4–5 inches. Test the temperature with your elbow or the inner side of your wrist. Undress your baby on a flat surface but leave his undershirt on. Clean the diaper area, then remove the undershirt. Wrap him in a towel so he doesn't panic at being undressed. Clean his eyes, ears and nose. Hold him with his legs under your armpit and your arm supporting his back. Fan out your fingers to cradle his head and lean over the bath to wash his head. Rinse well and pat dry. Remove the towel then hold him cradled in your hands and arms. Gently place him in the bath so that you are facing him. Keep him in a semi-upright position so that the lower half of his body is immersed and his head and shoulders are clear of the water. Use your free hand to wash him. You will probably find that he is quite slippery. Put a hand towel or large sponge mat in the bottom to stop him from slipping along the bath and to give you some control over his wriggling. Chat and smile to him all the time. When your

RIGHT AND OPPOSITE Bathtime can be an occasion for you to establish extra closeness with your baby. Make it a pleasant time, and chat and smile to your baby while you are washing him. Make as much body contact as possible, washing him gently but thoroughly. In time, most babies find baths very enjoyable and will splash around with pleasure.

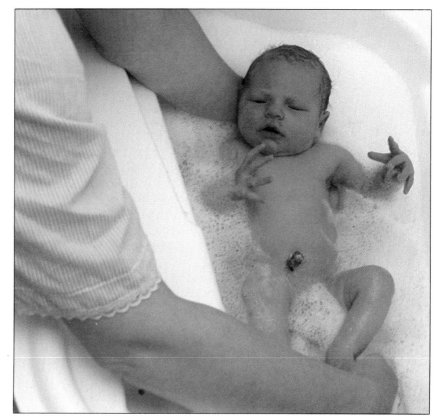

baby is clean and well-rinsed, put your free hand under his bottom and gently lift him onto a towel. Dry him carefully, especially his skin creases.

CRADLE CAP

Cradle cap is a form of baby dandruff of the scalp and consists of piles of dead scales which are normally shed from the scalp quite naturally due to daily wear and tear. The reason they are not shed from a baby's scalp is that the speed with which these keratin scales are made by a newborn baby's skin is much more rapid than an adult so they simply pile on top of one another. Daily brushing and shampooing of hair and scalp can help prevent cradle cap.

Along with the scales of dead skin there is a build up of grease which hardens the scales and they are difficult to rub off. If left for any length of time the scales dry out and become hard and encrusted. They should never be removed with your fingernails, because this could introduce infection.

Although there are a number of proprietary treatments on the market, it may be sufficient to gently massage the scales with cotton balls dipped in baby oil in the morning and wash the oil off with the nightly shampoo, then rinse. It may be necessary to repeat this morning and evening treatment to remove all the scales, but be slow and patient. Once the scalp is clear keep an eye out for the first signs of recurrence and apply the oil and shampoo treatment. If the condition is severe or does not clear up you should discuss it with your doctor.

You may find that your baby sweats around the head when he is sleeping. There is no need to worry and this sweating is of no significance.

STICKY EYE

You may notice that your baby develops a yellowish discharge at the inner corner of his eye. Known as "sticky eye", this is not always an indication of an infection, but usually a reaction to the amniotic fluid from your birth canal getting into his eye. Also, as newborn babies do not manufacture tears, they do not have the benefit of having the eye constantly bathed with this powerful, natural antiseptic lotion. Sticky eye is common in the first 48 hours of life.

You should carefully clean each eye with an individual dampened cotton ball. Take each cotton ball from the inside to the outside of each eye, only once, and then throw it away. With this routine, the sticky eye should be gone in two days. If it hasn't cleared, contact your doctor.

When laying your baby down, try to keep his unaffected eye on the side of the mattress. Otherwise, if the sticky eye comes in contact with the sheet it could contaminate the clear one when he turns over. You could put a gauze diaper over the sheet and replace it each time you go in to see him.

Sticky eye may be due also to bacterial infection, particularly if the discharge is heavy, and the eyes become red and swollen. Besides cleansing, an antibiotic ointment may be needed, so consult your doctor. Treatment is invariably effective and no permanent harm will come to your baby's eyes.

You will need to clean your baby's eyes with dampened cotton balls. Wipe from the inside of the eye to the outside, and use a fresh cotton ball for each eye. This helps to prevent any infection that might be present spreading from one eye to the other.

UMBILICAL CORD

Immediately after birth the umbilical cord is clamped with two clamps and cut with sterile scissors, leaving about a 2–3 inch length of cord protruding from your baby's stomach. The cord is then clamped about $\frac{1}{2}$–1

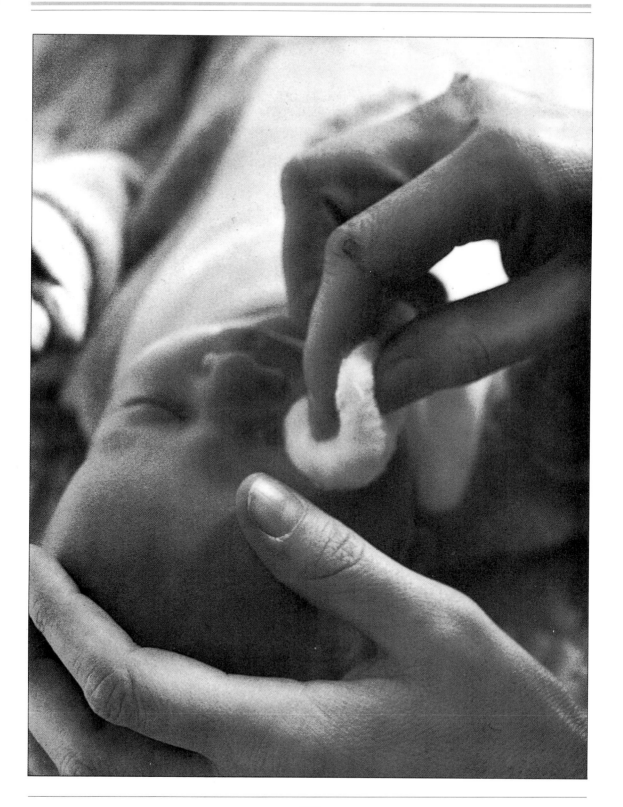

inch from the body with a pair of elastic bands or a tensioned plastic clip called a Hollister clamp. Over the next few days the cord dries and shrivels, and then drops off within about a week. To prevent that part of the cord attached to the baby's umbilicus (navel) from becoming infected you should clean it two to three times daily with alcohol and keep it dry and clean. The umbilicus should be treated in the same way after the cord has shrivelled and separated because there is still a slight risk of infection during the first few days.

Some babies develop umbilical hernias (small swellings of the navel) but these nearly always clear up within a year or two of their own accord. If your baby has one and it enlarges or persists consult your doctor.

Don't apply baby powder immediately after a bath if your baby is still damp. This can be very drying to the skin. Instead, allow your baby to dry thoroughly before applying any powder.

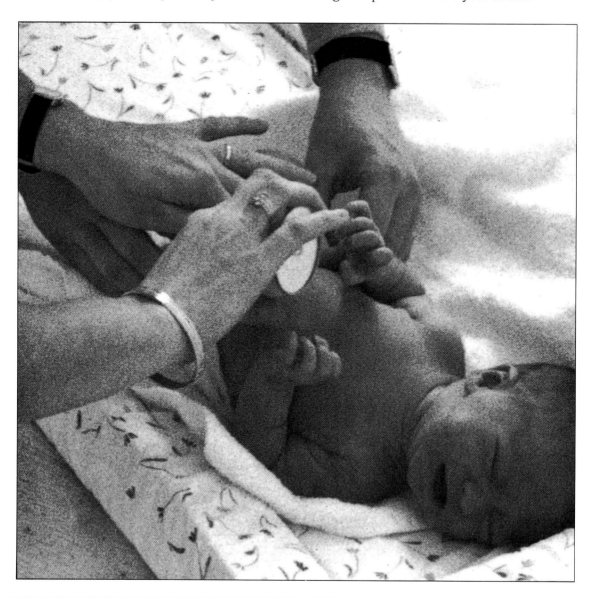

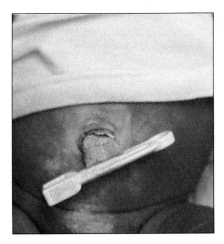

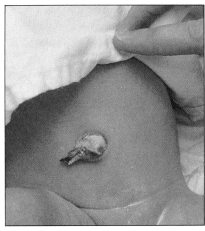

The umbilical cord needs no special care beyond keeping the area clean and dry to avoid the risk of infection. The cord will have been cut after delivery and a short stump left on, which may be clamped by a plastic clip. Let the area stay open to air as much as possible, by folding down the top of the diaper, if necessary, as this will help prevent moisture from wet diapers affecting the area.

NAILS

At birth the nails of the normal mature infant reach to the ends of the fingers. They are very soft and easily damaged if the baby grasps anything rough. They become quite firm in two to three days when your baby may scratch his face. If he scratches his face you can trim the edges of his nails with a baby scissors. This is best done when he is very sleepy so he won't move around much. It is recommended to cut them straight across then you can place loose-fitting mittens on his hands. Your baby may get an infection of the nail folds from sucking his fingers but this can also be prevented by putting cotton mittens on his hands for a few days.

CIRCUM-CISION

Your baby boy may be circumcised for religious reasons, in very rare cases because it is medically advisable, or simply because you wish it. If it is being done for religious reasons, circumcision usually takes place about the eighth day after birth. It is performed either by a doctor or a specially trained rabbi or lay person. If the baby is premature, jaundiced or has any other reason not to be fit for the operation, it is postponed until he is well enough.

In the U.S., circumcision is almost routinely performed by the obstetrician on the day after delivery. In other countries, such as Great Britain, most doctors do not recommend circumcision unless it is absolutely necessary. If you are going to have your baby circumcised, the operation should be done as soon as possible after the delivery, once your baby has established himself in a feeding routine and is gaining weight satisfactorily.

After circumcision, it is important to keep a careful watch during the first few hours to make sure the penis is not bleeding. The dressing is usually vasoline gauze, which is easily removed from the penis. If no dressing has been applied, you will be told how to bathe the baby and about special care of the penis. Whatever type of operation is performed, the penis is nearly always swollen and slightly inflamed for a few days, but if you treat it with care, it will gradually settle down. Occasionally, the penis may become irritated by his diaper and there may be a little blood; both are normal.

7

BEING AT HOME

The full realization of being a parent, and all that goes with it, probably doesn't occur until you arrive home, infant in arms. Up until that time you and your baby were in the care of the hospital's medical staff; now you have to assume total responsibility. The sudden shock of total responsibility can be overwhelming.

Even though you are filled with warm and loving feelings towards your baby, and have a strong desire to care for and protect her, you may find yourself worried by feelings of inadequacy and incompetence. In fact, you may feel as though you could do with some mothering, too. All these feelings are normal. We are not born with parenting abilities; we have to learn them by taking care of babies.

The important thing is to relax and follow your instincts. Don't become so concerned with getting things right that you allow yourself to become tense and anxious. Let your loving feelings guide you and you should find that your responses are the correct ones.

Don't hesitate to ask for help if you think you need it. It is surprising how much of your energy and time your new baby requires.

When it is time for you and your baby to leave the hospital, the doctor will examine both of you. Your breasts and uterus will be checked, and you will be given a date for your post-natal check-up or advised to see your doctor near that date. Your baby will be checked and this is a good time to ask any questions or discuss any worries you might have.

You should dress your baby warmly as she will not be efficient at regulating her body temperature. You should have some loose comfortable clothing available, as your breasts will have enlarged greatly when the milk comes in and your abdomen will not have gone down yet.

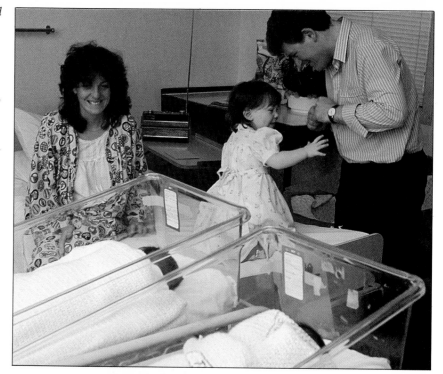

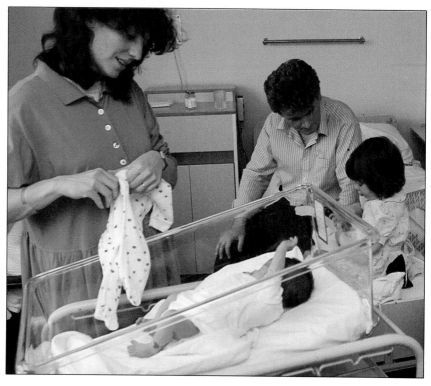

You should ensure that your partner is involved in caring for your newborn as much and as early as possible. This helps him to get used to the baby and prepares him for what is to come when the three of you arrive home. It also includes him in a process that often only involves the mother and baby.

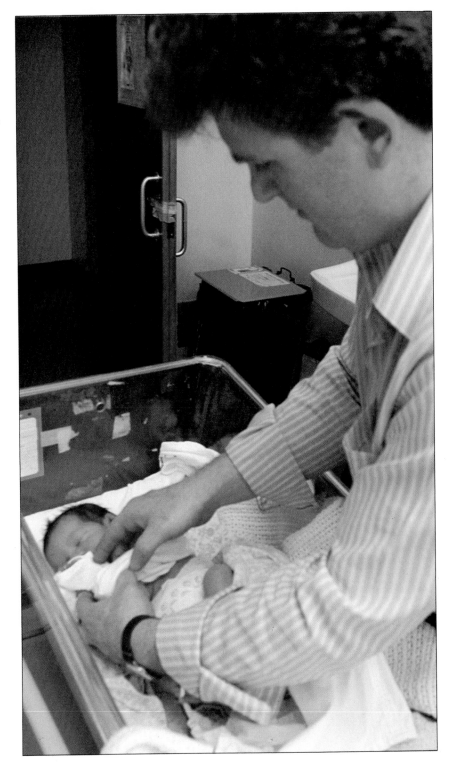

Once your baby is home you can safely remove her identification bracelet. Make sure that your baby's room is warm enough; ideally it should be kept constant at about 75°F. Babies love to look at things, so have some brightly colored posters or mobiles hanging above where she will sleep.

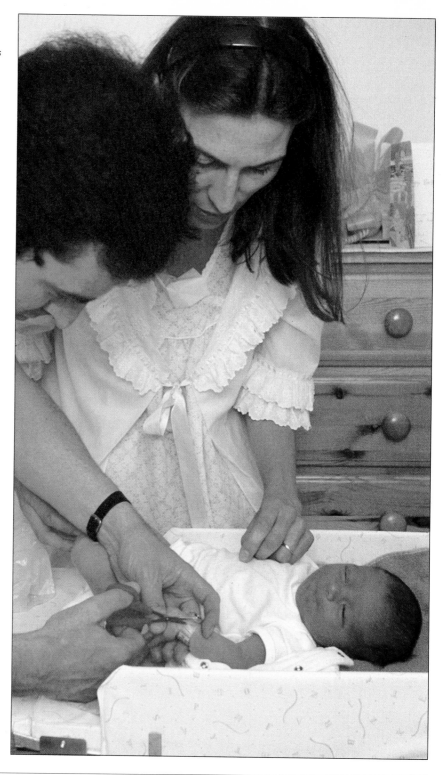

BABY'S ROOM AND EQUIPMENT

It is not essential for your baby to have her own room right away, and many parents prefer to keep newborns in their bedrooms to make feeding easier and nights less broken and more restful. But, if you have the space, do equip it before you come home from the hospital. This room should have everything you need for the daily routines such as changing, feeding, playing and dressing. The room should have lots of light and look bright and cheerful. Babies love bright primary colors, so try to include some in the color scheme. There is no reason you have to stick to pastels. When choosing paint, make sure it is nontoxic and lead free. You might also consider wallpapers or borders designed specifically for children's rooms.

You will need lots of storage and shelving; encourage your do-it-yourself partner. Simple shelving that is open is better than drawers and cupboards — you can see everything at a glance. Make sure it is hygienic and easy to wipe clean. Keep the items you use regularly within easy reach. You may wish to leave the storage spaces open, but doors will need to be put on later when the baby is mobile.

Make sure the room has a night-light or install a dimmer switch; you don't want it completely dark when she awakens at night nor do you want bright lights in your baby's eyes during night-time feeds and changing. Dim light helps the baby to get back to sleep more quickly.

You can choose between a cradle or a crib for the baby to sleep in. A cradle is not really necessary, and you can put the baby into a crib straight away. Ensure it has a special baby mattress, which is firm and covered with waterproof material. Do not get a pillow, at least for the first year, as babies might suffocate in the fabric covers. Choose toweling or flannelette sheets for warmth, and make sure you have about four to six on hand. You will also need a blanket or a baby duvet. A blanket may be a better choice at first, as babies can sometimes feel lost under a duvet. Babies love to watch things that move so try to include a hanging mobile over the crib.

A baby bath isn't essential as the baby can be bathed in the kitchen or bathroom sink. But if you choose to have one make sure it is made of firm plastic. Get a couple of new soft bath towels that are specifically for the baby's use. You might also want to get a natural sponge or some soft wash-cloths for the baby as well.

You will need to get a plastic changing mat and have a bag full of the changing supplies, such as cotton balls, petroleum jelly, baby soap, cream, baby wipes and cornstarch baby powder. You may want to get a changing bag, which makes carrying the supplies around that much easier.

When choosing a baby carriage, there are so many options that it is best to figure out your own needs and then look for the one that suits. As they are expensive, you might consider borrowing one or buying secondhand if you find one in good condition. A carrying sling or backpack is useful for the first six months or so, and keeps the baby close to you and your partner. If you have a car, the law requires you to have a car seat for the baby. The car seat can be secured by seatbelts.

HELPING HER TO SLEEP

Your baby can sleep anywhere as long as she's warm and comfortable. Warmth is important, as babies don't have full control over their body temperatures and lose heat very quickly. In the first few weeks it is advisable not to lay your baby on her back just in case she vomits some of her feed and inhales some of the curds. Put your baby down on her front or side. Even though your baby will follow her own sleep pattern it is important that she learns to differentiate between night and day. There are several ways of helping your baby to do this. For example, when putting your baby down in the evening make sure the room is darkened and make an extra effort to ensure she is comfortable and contented. When she wakes to be fed in the night simply give the feed but don't play or otherwise distract your baby, or she will not go back to sleep easily, and it may prove difficult to reduce night feeds later. During the night, feed your baby as soon as she cries. If you leave her to cry herself to sleep, she will only wake again later, extremely hungry, when you have just managed to go to sleep yourself. As she gets older and more aware of what's going on, you can develop an evening routine, waking your baby for a late-night feed at your own bedtime.

There is no doubt you will be tired and need to get as much rest as possible. Try to sleep when the baby does, as when she wakes up she will undoubtedly need feeding and changing. Even if you cannot get to sleep, lying quietly will help.

If possible, ask other members of the family to help with the baby so that you do not get too exhausted to cope. If you try to maintain the lifestyle you had previously, without any additional help, this may put even more pressure on you and you might feel incapable of doing anything well. Without help, you are just going to have to let certain things go. Perhaps your home isn't as neat and tidy as it once was but what is important is that you spend the available time on your baby and yourself.

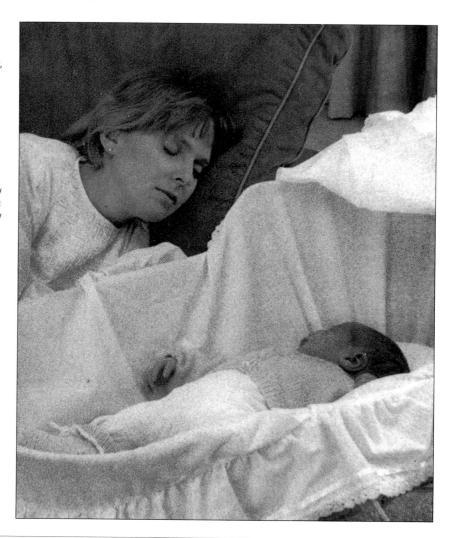

BREAST CARE

When you are breastfeeding it is important to take good care of your breasts to avoid soreness and cracking. Buy good maternity bras, and wear them for support. Get properly measured and buy ones that fit you properly. Bras that have a drop front are good because they ensure the breast is rapidly available. Make sure the bras offer good support underneath the breasts without cutting into the shoulders.

Daily hygiene includes cleansing breasts and nipples every day with water or baby lotion. Don't use soap because it dries the skin and can aggravate a sore or cracked nipple. Handle your breasts carefully. Pat them gently dry after both feeding and washing. Leave nipples to dry in open air whenever you can. A little lanolin may help cracked skin but be sure to wipe it off with water before feeding. You can still wear a bra, but keep the front flaps down. You might find that milk leaks during the day. If so, put breast pads inside your bra to soak up the leaking milk. Change the breast pads often.

Engorged breasts

Breasts commonly become heavy and hard on the third or fourth day after childbirth, when the milk first comes in. Later on they may also become overfull of milk. The following can help make feeding easier if they do become engorged:

- Bathe breasts in warm water before feeds. Gently stroking breasts firmly towards nipple for a few moments also helps ease the tenderness.
- You can express a little milk to relieve some of the heaviness.
- Wear a firm support bra.

Sore nipples

Sore nipples may occur in the first few weeks if your baby is a strong or vigorous sucker or if you take her roughly off your breasts and if the nipple is not right at the back of her mouth. Keep trying to feed but change your position frequently. Expose your nipples to warm air or sunlight by leaving the feeding flaps down. Don't use soap or cotton balls to clean your nipples and let them dry off naturally in between feeds. There are also various creams and sprays on the market for treating sore nipples.

Cracked nipples

Cracked nipples occur for a variety of reasons most of which are avoidable. The crack usually appears where the nipple joins the areola. If treated promptly it will heal quickly. Take your baby off your breast for up to 72 hours if the nipple is actually cracked. You will probably need to express milk manually or by a breast pump to keep up the production of milk.

Blocked ducts

If you have blocked ducts, your breasts will fell lumpy and tender where the blockage is. Try starting a couple of feeds with the blocked breast until the blockage clears. When your baby is sucking, gently stroke over the lumpy area with your fingertips, smoothing the milk towards the nipple. If the blockage doesn't clear and the skin of the breast becomes red, shiny, hot and sore, or if you feel feverish, check your temperature and see your doctor. This way you will avoid a breast abscess.

EXERCISES

After the birth you will gradually feel better as you find your routine and become more active. Exercising after pregnancy is important, in particular to help the muscles of your back, abdomen and pelvic floor, and to increase

At first you may find it easier to ignore schedules and nurse on demand. Your baby will know when she is hungry. On average, most newborns nurse approximately every two hours, and many feed more frequently at home than while in the hospital.

There is no need to eat or avoid special foods while feeding, although you may want to avoid large amounts of caffeine and alcohol. However, you may find that your baby nurses less strongly or develops gas after you have eaten strongly-flavored foods.

circulation. The muscles in the abdomen return quickly, providing that not too much weight has been gained, and that proper exercises are performed. Pelvic floor exercises are also important, but if you had stitches or a tear you may be a bit sore to start them immediately. The way to ease it is to smear some antiseptic cream onto your stitches to soften the skin and then try to exercise gently. You should do your pelvic exercises every time you pass urine (for the rest of your life) to tighten up your vagina, the other pelvic organs and their supporting ligaments, at least once a day as soon as you can manage after delivery.

Your doctor can provide you with special booklets and instructions for exercising your other muscles. Imagine the pelvic floor is a lift, stopping at various levels. Aim to contract the muscles gradually in five stages with a short stop at each, not letting go between the levels. Then allow the pelvic floor to descend, releasing the contraction level by level. When you reach the starting point, allow the muscles to relax completely so that you feel a

Your newborn won't be ready for toys for some weeks but when you put her down, for instance while you do your exercises, she will find the soft fur of a teddy very comforting.

slight bulging down. It is better to exercise for short periods of time, say five minutes a few times a day, rather than in one long stretch. Do the exercises slowly and rest briefly between exercises. And don't overdo it. Stop when you are tired. These exercises are most effective if started shortly after birth – within the first few weeks.

INFECTION

There are various infections you might develop after childbirth. A fever on the third or fourth day after delivery, when you could already be at home, could possibly be a sign of postpartum infection or it could be caused by a virus or other minor problem. A low-grade fever of about 100°F, or even higher, can occasionally accompany engorgement when your milk first comes in.

In postpartum infection, symptoms vary according to the site affected. A slight fever, vague lower abdominal pain and perhaps foul-smelling vaginal discharge characterise endometritis, an infection of the endometrium (the lining of the uterus). The endometrium is vulnerable because of detachment

RIGHT
Usually on the third day after birth your baby will have a special blood or urine test. This is to test for phenylketonuria (PKU), a metabolic disorder which leads to brain damage if left untreated. If PKU is present your baby is put on a special diet which prevents damage occurring.

OPPOSITE
Feeling at ease with your baby means that you can care for her in a way that suits your lifestyle. Rather than rushing off to change her in her room, you can make do with what you have at hand and many mothers soon learn the trick of doing more than one thing at a time.

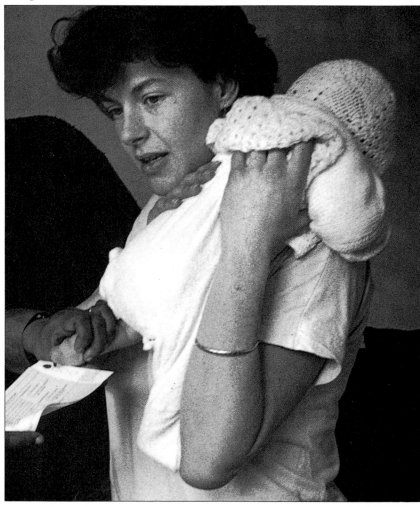

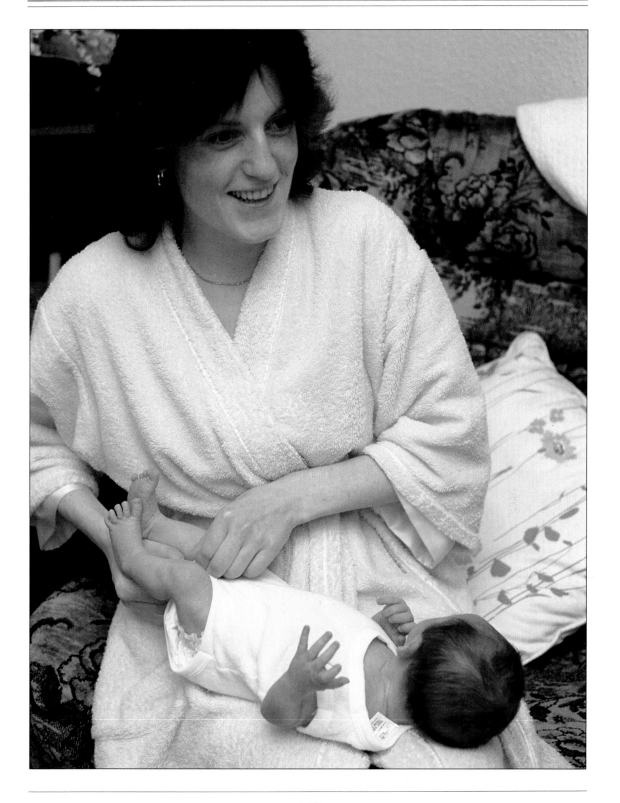

of the placenta and the open cervix from the delivery. Infection is even more likely to occur here if a fragment of the placenta has been retained.

Perineal infection may occur if there is some tear or laceration, including an episiotomy. It may begin around the stitches or the tear. Infection in the stitches usually does not have any lasting effect, and is relieved when they are removed. It clears up quickly but there is sometimes a slight discharge for several days or even weeks after the stitches have been removed.

Breast infections are rare during pregnancy but more common after delivery and during lactation. This shouldn't be confused with engorgement. The breasts normally become engorged the third or fourth day after delivery which may be associated with a slight rise in temperature, but no infection is present. Breast infection occurs in a specific area of the breast and is usually preceded by a crack in the nipple. Or, a red sore lump on the breast may indicate a clogged duct that can lead to infection. The first sign of infection is usually a sharp rise in temperature, with a rise in pulse rate. This may be accompanied by flushing or reddening of the skin over the affected part of the breast, which will be tender to touch and also rather engorged.

Report any fever during the first three weeks to your doctor, even if it is accompanied by obvious symptoms of cold or flu, so that it can be diagnosed and treatment with antibiotics started.

If you have another child at home you already will have prepared him or her for the new arrival. To help keep any sibling rivalry in bounds, remind your firstborn, as you care for the new baby, that you once did all this for him or her. You could say, too, that the reason you had another child was because he or she is so terrific.

Once your baby is home you will need to introduce her to other members of the family. If the baby's grandparents are with you try to include them in your routine as much as possible. Encourage them to hold and cuddle the new baby, as she loves all physical closeness and body contact. You may also find your relatives an invaluable source of support and knowledge about aspects of baby care and behavior.

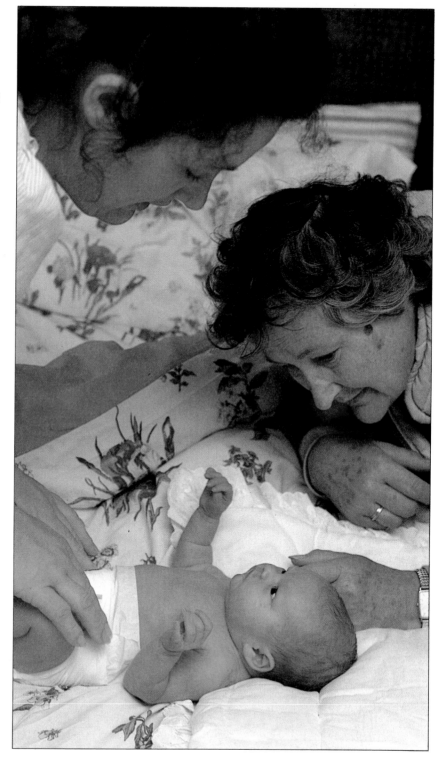

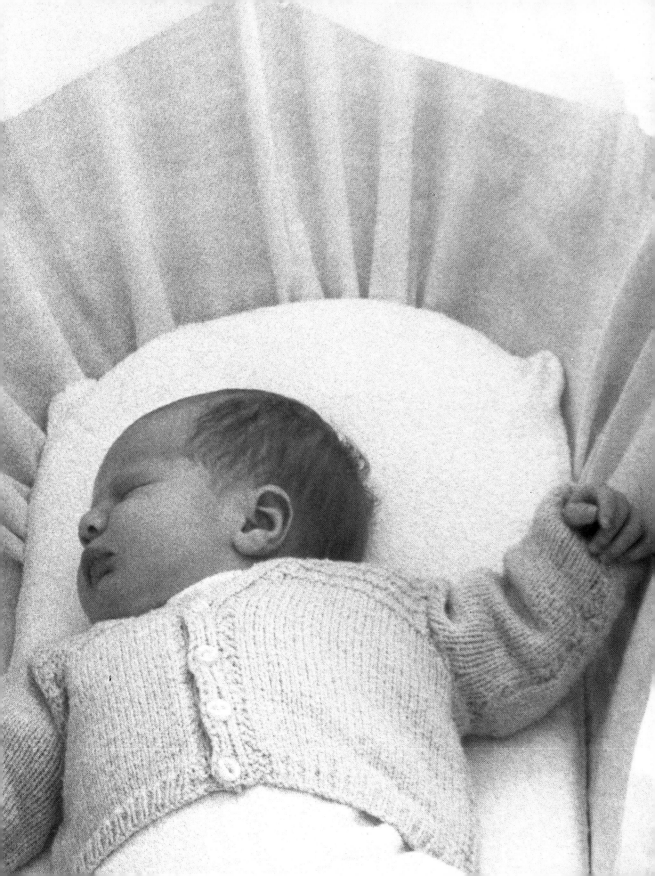

REST AND RELAXATION

Resting is just as important as exercising. You need to recover from the exertions of labor and delivery to manage all your new responsibilities. Try sleeping when your baby does and, while you are holding and feeding her, sit down with your feet up. Lie down and rest at least twice a day.

SIX WEEK CHECK-UP

You will have a routine check-up six or eight weeks after delivery. At this time you can discuss any problems you have, with either your own health or your baby's. If you had a cesarean, your doctor may also check your incision sooner. Doctor's examinations vary, but should include:

● Taking your blood pressure
● Checking your weight, which should be down by 17–20lb
● Examining the shape, size and location of your uterus, to see if it has returned to its pre-pregnant condition and location
● Checking the condition of the cervix and vagina and examining any episiotomy or laceration repair site for healing
● Doing a pap smear
● Examining the breasts
● Discussing contraception

Coping with a new baby can be very demanding. Don't hesitate to ask for help if your family, friends or neighbors offer it or appear willing to do so. This will enable you to have a break from the chores and responsibilities and also to catch up on your sleep.

Being a new mother, you will find that people offer all sorts of advice. Some of it may be helpful, but there is no need to follow it if you do not feel comfortable. Don't be embarrassed to discuss any problems with your doctor instead of relying on helpful friends and neighbors.

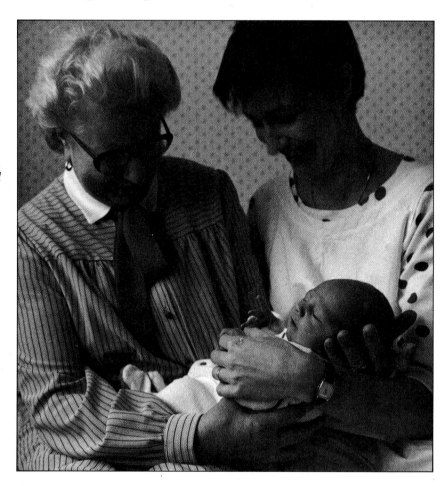

SLEEPING EQUIPMENT

A bassinet or cradle is attractive to look at but is not very economical, as your baby will soon outgrow it. A crib will last your baby longest, especially if it converts to a toddler bed. Choose a drop-sided one that will allow you to pick up and put down your baby easily. For your baby's safety, make certain the crib slats are no more than 2⅜in (62mm) apart. The mattress you buy should be firmly sprung and fit snugly. Protect it with a waterproof covering. If you use a protective bumper, trim the excess length from the attaching ribbons and always tie them firmly. Your baby can choke on loose ends that may fall into the crib. Fitted sheets are easier to use than flat sheets; the latter must have their ends tucked in well. For a covering, use only a continental quilt or closely woven blanket without fringes. Your baby should not have a pillow.

CHECKLIST
- ☐ Crib, cradle or bassinet
- ☐ Bumpers for crib
- ☐ Mattress
- ☐ Waterproof sheet
- ☐ Top sheet
- ☐ Continental quilt or cellular blanket

Padded basket with hood

Wooden rocking cradle

Fitted sheet

Tie-on waterproof sheet

Pushable bassinet

Slatted wooded crib with drop sides and adjustable mattress

Cellular blanket

Flame-proof washable continental quilt

Foam safety mattress with indents to prevent suffocation

Firmly sprung horsehair mattress

OUTINGS

A sling allows you to take your newborn everywhere with you. A large full-size baby carriage is not as practical as one with a collapsible frame, although both must have good brakes, safety harness rings, and be easy to push. For newborns, only lie-back strollers are suitable. At all times, a baby must be in a car seat when traveling in a car.

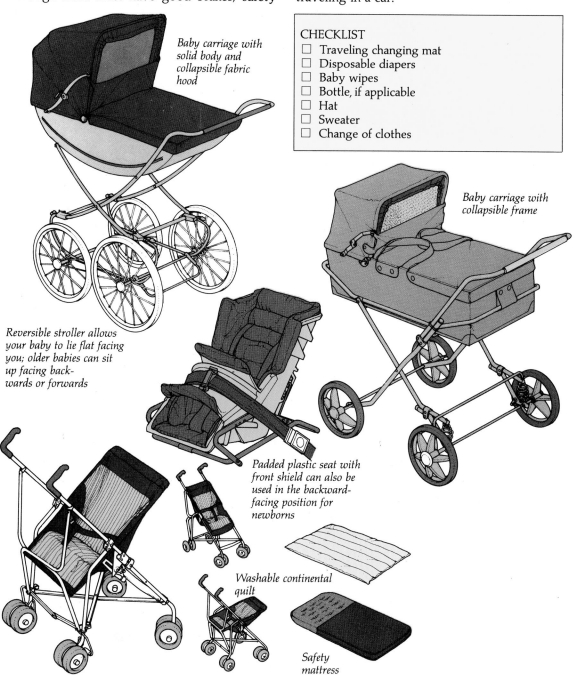

Baby carriage with solid body and collapsible fabric hood

CHECKLIST
- ☐ Traveling changing mat
- ☐ Disposable diapers
- ☐ Baby wipes
- ☐ Bottle, if applicable
- ☐ Hat
- ☐ Sweater
- ☐ Change of clothes

Baby carriage with collapsible frame

Reversible stroller allows your baby to lie flat facing you; older babies can sit up facing backwards or forwards

Padded plastic seat with front shield can also be used in the backward-facing position for newborns

Washable continental quilt

Safety mattress

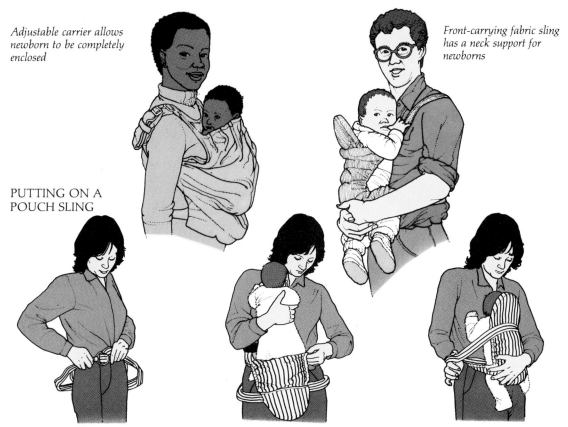

Adjustable carrier allows newborn to be completely enclosed

Front-carrying fabric sling has a neck support for newborns

PUTTING ON A POUCH SLING

Clip the sling on around your waist then swivel the fixing to the back

Pick up your baby and, holding her steady, maneuver her legs into the leg holes with your free hand

Pull one side of the sling up over your baby and on to your shoulder. Swap hands and repeat with the other side, all the time keeping a firm hold

PUTTING ON AN ENCLOSED SLING

LEANING FORWARDS
Always cradle your baby's head if you have to lean forwards or stretch over to one side

Put on the sling as the instructions direct. Open the zippers and slip your baby comfortably onto the inner seat. Zip up the seat section

With one hand still supporting your baby, pull the outer cover around her and do up the outer zipper

INDEX